BRADY

Brady Minton's trouble was that he couldn't keep a secret. He just naturally had to tell everything he knew.

After all, there were so many interesting things to talk about: his brother, Matt, had just been appointed a professor of history; his friend Ranger knew where the best trout fishing was; and something strange was going on at Drover Hull's cabin.

That's what really started the trouble. He suspected that Drover Hull was helping runaway slaves, so he told his father. The minute he did he regretted it. He could tell by the look on his father's face that he had opened his mouth once too often. When he learned that his father had a part in the slavery issue, Brady wanted to help, but he knew his father didn't trust him to keep a secret.

Jean Fritz has written a sympathetic, moving story of a young boy in pre–Civil War days, who was forced to make his own decision on the question of slavery and who learned how important it can be to keep a secret.

BRADY

by Jean Fritz

Illustrated by Lynd Ward

Puffin Books

PUFFIN BOOKS
Published by the Penguin Group
Penguin Books USA Inc.,
375 Hudson Street, New York, New York 10014, U.S.A.
Penguin Books Ltd, 27 Wrights Lane, London W8 5TZ, England
Penguin Books Australia Ltd, Ringwood, Victoria, Australia
Penguin Books Canada Ltd, 10 Alcorn Avenue, Toronto, Ontario, Canada M4V 3B2
Penguin Books (N.Z.) Ltd, 182–190 Wairau Road, Auckland 10, New Zealand

Penguin Books Ltd, Registered Offices: Harmondsworth, Middlesex, England

First published by Coward, McCann & Geoghegan, Inc., 1960
Published in Puffin Books 1987
Copyright © Jean Fritz, 1960

16 18 20 19 17 15

Library of Congress Cataloging-in-Publication Data
Fritz, Jean.   Brady.
Originally published: New York: Coward-McCann, 1960.
Summary: A young Pennsylvania boy takes part in the
pre-Civil War anti-slavery activities.
[1. Slavery—Fiction.   2. Pennsylvania—Fiction]
[I. Ward, Lynd, 1905– ill.   II. Title.   PZ7.F919Br
1987   [Fic]   87-14555   ISBN 0-14-032258-2

Although a few of the incidents in this book are based on actual happenings, the characters and the story are purely imaginary, reflecting only the spirit of the day.

This book is for the Mintons, the Hannas, the Scotts and all the families who settled Washington County and for their children's children. Most particularly, it is for two of those children — David Minton Fritz and Andrea Scott Fritz.

For help in the preparation of this book, I wish to thank my parents, Mr. and Mrs. Arthur Minton Guttery, and my husband, Michael Fritz. I am also very much indebted to Margaret Swart, Elizabeth and Holland Weir, Earle R. Forrest, and Blanche Ferguson.

BRADY

Chapter One

BRADY MINTON sat down on the back steps to enjoy
the good feeling inside him. There wasn't a single
thing he *had* to do all afternoon. Not a single thing, he
told himself. If he wanted, he could go on sitting here
for hours, watching the white clouds sleep in the June
sky. He could lean back lazy on his elbows and smell
the turkey roasting in the kitchen and listen to his

grandmother's voice laughing and saying "Pee-*pul*!" the way she always did when she was tickled over something. Brady loved the way she said it, coasting along slow on the first part of "people," then slamming down hearty on the second. You could feel the whole world all at once in his grandmother's expression and you loved it and laughed at it in the same way she did.

"Pee-*pul*!" Brady repeated to himself and grinned. Well, it was a good world that gave him an afternoon like this and a brother like Matt, who was the cause for the holiday-ing. They had heard the good news about Matt last week, that he had been appointed Professor of History at nearby Washington College, the youngest man to receive such an appointment. Professor Minton. That's what Brady would call him when Matt got home this evening. "How do you do, Professor?" he'd say. And then Matt would grin and maybe punch him in the ribs and say, "Hello there, Snapper." Once in a while Matt still called Brady by the nickname they'd all used years ago when Brady had kept an old mud turtle as a pet.

One thing was sure. If it weren't for Matt's becoming a professor, Brady wouldn't be where he was right now. He'd be out in the fields or chopping wood or doing chores of one sort or another. He was the only young one on the farm now. Since his Aunt Nell had died several months ago, his Uncle Earl was living with them and, of course, there was his girl, Mary Dorcas. But she was only ten years old and everyone thought she was too pretty to lend a hand outdoors. It was surprising how many things a body could get out of by being a girl and how many things a mother and a father and an uncle could think of to keep a boy busy. Especially when the father was a preacher and the uncle a sheriff and they ran a small farm besides. Sometimes it seemed to Brady that the sight of him sitting down was enough to suggest another odd job that needed attending to. But this morning they had gone off, his mother and father and Uncle Earl, and for a wonder no one had thought to outline any special afternoon work for him. They had taken the buggy and gone to Washington College to attend the reception being given Matt and then to fetch him home. The reception was to be at the home of Reverend McConaughy, the president of the college, and all the faculty would be there and the trustees and important people from all over the county. Professor Matthew Minton. Brady couldn't get used to the grandness of it.

Well, there would be a reception of sorts at home tonight too. Brady's grandmother and Aunt Sadie and Uncle Will had driven down from the next county north to be here when Matt got home. His grandmother and Aunt Sadie were already at work on dinner, which was going to be a regular Thanksgiving affair, judging from the conversation and the smells in the kitchen. Mary Dorcas was in there helping or pretending to help, but Brady and his Uncle Will had been shooed out and told not to get underfoot. Uncle Will had gone to the front porch to read the paper and Brady had dropped down here on the back stoop.

It wasn't often that Brady had time like this to turn his mind loose and let it take him where it pleased. From thinking about Matt, Brady started to think about himself. Not about himself today or tomorrow — he knew that self well enough — but about the strange grown-up self he supposed he would become. Several times recently he'd caught his father looking at him as if he were trying to picture Brady's grown-up self. Brady guessed that was natural enough. Since his oldest brother, Luke, had become a farmer, married and moved to Ohio, only Brady was left now with his future unaccounted for. He pushed his bare feet through a stubble of weeds at the bottom of the steps until he could feel the warm earth beneath. Well, there was no telling. Maybe he'd make his family proud of him the way they were of Matt. And maybe he wouldn't.

In any case, all of that was too far away to think about now. Today was June 10, 1836; the afternoon was green and golden and rolling with hills as far as he could see. In Pennsylvania, the land could never lie flat for more than a few minutes at a time; it rose and fell as if it had breath and life of its own. The Minton farm was at the top of one of the hills and when you looked at the world from there, it was hard to remember there was anything wrong with it. Hard to believe, Brady thought, there was such a thing as the sin his father preached about or slavery that set people so against each other. Brady leaned over and picked up his cat, which had come crying out of the kitchen. Poor old Catfish. In a world that looked so good on the outside, it didn't even seem right that Catfish had to be unhappy. She'd been walking around crying ever since her two kittens had taken some sort of fit day before last and died, both of them. She would look in the box behind the stove and see it empty; then she'd set up wailing louder than ever. Brady rubbed his face against her fur, then set her down on the top step.

"Never mind, Catfish," he said. "Instead of grieving over your last kittens, you sit here in the sun and start thinking about your next ones. I'm going down to the hollow and see what Range is up to."

It was a sure thing that his friend, Range Hadley, wouldn't be doing any chores today, Brady thought, nor Range's father either. Most people said Mr. Hadley was kind of no-account and even though his wife was dead, he should be ashamed to bring up a boy the way he did Range, letting him do as he pleased, never sending him to church or school unless he asked to go. But Brady didn't know about that. All he knew was that there weren't two people in the world who seemed to have a better time than Range and his father. Thinking about them now, Brady hurried down the hill, past the new cornfield, and then through the pasture cluttered with stumps still waiting to be dug up.

When Brady came to the goat shed, he stopped to look as he always did. Of course it hadn't been a goat shed for some time. When they had stopped keeping goats, Brady's father had turned the shed into what he called his Sermon House. It was where he went to study and pray and write his sermons. And it was private. No one else had been inside since his father had fixed it up, drawn the curtain, and locked the door. Brady put his face up against the window, thinking that maybe this time the curtain might be pulled aside. But it wasn't and he walked on, wondering again. Sometimes Brady almost had the feeling that God Himself must be locked up inside his father's mysterious Sermon House, and if he could only get a peek through the window, he would understand the world a lot better.

Brady climbed over the pasture fence and now he could see Range's house down there in the hollow and Miller's Creek running past it. The house wasn't much more than a shack backed up by a white oak tree, but what Brady liked about it was its porch, wider than the house itself, sagging at the steps where it was most used, and littered with the tag ends of the Hadleys' days — fishing gear, whittling sticks, pheasants hanging by their feet from the rafters, scraps of inventions that Mr. Hadley and Range were always working on, a couple of half-finished chairs. Whenever the Hadleys ran low on supplies, Mr. Hadley made a chair and sold it. He was handy that way and could have made a good living at his chairs, but he'd rather do other things.

As Brady came closer, he grinned. Range and his father were sitting on the porch railing, their feet dangling over the outside edge, and they were fishing. From where they sat, they were throwing their lines clean into Miller's Creek.

"Hey there," Brady called. "You fellows catching or are you getting caught?"

Range reached for a string of trout hanging on the railing and held it up for Brady to see.

"Find yourself a line, Brady," Mr. Hadley boomed, "and come roost up here with us a spell. Ought to be a line on the porch somewheres."

Brady walked up to the porch, stepping over a litter of young pigs and making his way past a table spilling over with odd pieces of Mr. Hadley's inventions. You couldn't tell what Mr. Hadley was working on now, but it didn't matter. After a few days he'd put these materials away and start on something else. Brady couldn't think of a thing Mr. Hadley had finished inventing, but he surely had a lot of ideas.

Brady picked up a fishing line and took his place on the railing. As he leaned against the porch post he thought again how nice it was down here with the trees marching a hundred strong and more on the other side of the creek. And now there was a redbird whistling from the top of one of the trees. If there was one thing that Brady was partial to, it was a redbird.

He fingered the fishing line, adjusting it until it was a comfortable coil in his left hand. With his right hand he made a few practice gestures and then swung the line into the air. He leaned forward, watching to see how it would come down on the water. But it never came down at all. Before he realized what was happening, a trout jumped up and swallowed the hook and in the same swift movement, dived for the bottom. The quick jerk of the line brought Brady sprawling to the ground. He landed on his stomach, his arms stretched in front of him and his legs spraddled, froglike, behind.

Behind him he could hear Range and Mr. Hadley laughing. "Hold 'er, boy," Mr. Hadley called. "She's a-rearin'!"

That's right, hold on, Brady told himself. Keep the line taut. Gradually he worked himself from his stomach, to his knees, to his feet, pulling in hand over hand whenever he could and at the same time making his way to the bank. There. There it was. Out of the water. A whopper.

"It's a big one!" Mr. Hadley roared his approval.

Range was still laughing as Brady came back to the porch. "Never dreamed you'd get one on the first throw. Next time hook your feet around the rail."

"Next time," Brady agreed, smiling. His eyes were still on his trout. A really good-sized one, he told himself. Maybe he could catch another to go with it. But by the time he had it strung and was ready to take his place on the rail again, Range had other ideas.

"Aw, let's not fish any more," Range said. "Let's go in the woods. I found a big patch of wild strawberries the other day over by Drover Hull's place."

Well, that was the way Range was. You'd get going on one idea and then he'd switch to another. But his ideas, Brady admitted, were nearly always good. It would be nice to walk through the woods today. Besides, he hadn't been over by Drover Hull's place for a long time. He always liked to creep up through the trees the way you had to and look at that little house set in

16

the middle of the woods with its vegetable garden spread out so neat behind it. You had to be very quiet because it would never do to let Drover Hull catch you peeking. A hermit didn't like to have people come snooping anywhere near. Still, you could stand behind a tree and watch the smoke curl up from Drover's chimney and if you were lucky, catch a glimpse of Drover himself. And all the time you would wonder what makes a man a hermit, what it is like.

Brady dropped his line on the porch. "Let's go;" he agreed. He was thinking so much about Drover Hull and wild strawberries that it didn't occur to him that Range had anything else in mind. He didn't notice Range going into the house until all at once he was back again with a rifle in each hand.

"As long as we're going in the woods," Range said, "we might as well see what we can shoot. You can take Pa's old gun."

Usually Brady had more of a chance to set his face so it would look right and no one would guess his secret. Usually he had a smile ready and acted as eager as the next one. But the fact was he hated to hunt, especially at this time of year when all the animals and birds of the woods were busy with their young. Oh, he was ashamed of himself, all right. It was unmanly and weak to feel this way. Weak, weak, he told himself over and over. He didn't want anyone to guess, particularly not Range Hadley, who was known all around for his marksmanship. And after all, how else would a boy get so he could shoot a running rabbit or a flying bird unless he had a lot of practice, never mind whether he always used what he shot or not?

Brady reached for the gun. "Sure," he said. "On a day like this, we might get a squirrel or two."

Chapter Two

THERE WAS ONE THING about Range. He knew better than anyone how to be quiet in the woods. Today, of course, he had his gun and any hunter would try to be quiet, but even without his gun Range was quiet, not like some boys Brady knew. Brady recalled the times he and Laban Williams had come to the woods together after school. Laban always raced around, foolish as a chicken, crackling twigs under his feet and hollering, "Looka here, looka here!" As if there would be anything to see after the fuss Laban had stirred up! Then after carrying on like this, Laban would tell some of his wild stories about the time he'd met a bear in the woods or the time he'd come upon a wolf. What's more, he'd tell it as if he expected you to believe it and tell it loud enough for all the animals in Washington County to hear. And all the time he'd be snapping that big jack-knife of his — open and shut, open and shut.

But Range, now — he knew that in the woods you walked and talked differently. He knew just where and how to put his feet down, when to hold still, when to slide on. When you were with Range, you had the feeling you were seeing the woods the way they *really* were. The way they looked when you weren't there. That is, of course, unless Range had his gun along and fired it. Right now he was loping along easy, letting the squirrels chatter overhead, pausing to watch a snake slip under some leaves. Then he stopped for a moment to let Brady catch up.

"Let's not shoot at anything," Range said, "till we're on the way back. The sound of a gun would carry over to Drover Hull's place and likely send him inside. If we can, I'd kind of like to get a peek at him. See what he's doin'."

Brady grinned. "Suits me." He let his steps fall in beside Range's. The sunlight, sifting down through the trees, made a lacy pattern for them to walk over.

"What do you suppose makes Drover want to live so wild?" Brady asked.

Range shrugged. "Maybe he's crazy in the head. Or maybe it's true what some folks say. You know, about his mother being a witch and all."

Brady thought of some of the stories he'd heard about Drover. He remembered the time several years back when Laban Williams and a group of boys had thrown rocks at Drover Hull's house and the next day every one of them had come down with a fever. Then there was another time when several of the neighbors' cows had died of hair balls. Some people around town who still remembered the old days after the War of Independence when there were more witches around said that old Drover Hull had learned from his mother the knack of shooting hair balls into the stomachs of cows. Of course Brady's grandmother and his pa said that was a lot of nonsense; Drover was only an old man who liked his own company. But Brady didn't know.

"Think he could cast a spell on you if he saw you?" Brady asked.

"I don't aim to have him see me." Range stepped around a giant oak that had been blown down in some unknown storm years back. The splintered ends of the broken trunk stood up ragged and sharp as if they still remembered the creaking and groaning of the falling tree.

Today all Brady could hear in the woods was Miller's Creek, turned back on its own course, rumbling through the trees. He couldn't see it but he could picture it, squeezing through the heavy growth and tangle of branches at times, at other times running free through a clearing with room enough and to spare.

Range put his nose in the air the same way a deer does to find out what the wind is bringing. "Smell anything?" he asked.

Brady grinned. He could smell it, all right. Strawberries. There must be a thousand of them to carry on the air like this. Then all at once almost without warning the trees gave way and Brady and Range were standing in a sunny clearing by the creek. The ground was covered with wild strawberries.

"Didn't I tell you?" Range began picking right away, stooping down and filling an old sack he had slung on his back. "Put your pickings in here," he said. "When we get home, we can divide up."

The strawberries were so plentiful, you could stand in one spot and pick them by the handful. And didn't they taste good, Brady thought, popping one into his mouth. There was nothing that tasted and smelled so much of June and new life in the ground as strawberries did. Later in the summer and fall, fruit seemed to have a heavier flavor, stronger and older somehow. Peaches, apples, grapes.

In no time at all, it seemed, the sack was heavy with berries, and that was enough, Range decided. From then on he and Brady ate what they picked, not one at a time but eight or ten in a mouthful, until their faces and hands were stained red and the juice was running down the front of their shirts.

Brady smiled at Range. "You're a sight to see," he said. "You look as if you'd been in a fight."

Range wiped his arm across his mouth. "Guess we better wash up."

Even their bare feet were red, they noticed, as they walked down to the creek. The ground was softer here, even muddy in places. In shady spots there were still a few late violets in bloom. There was something else too. As Range leaned over to slap water on his face, he noticed at the edge of the creek a large man-sized footprint.

"Somebody's been here kind of recently," Range said. He rinsed his hands and face quickly and looked at the footprint again. "A big man with heavy boots. He wasn't alone, either."

Beside the first footprints Range and Brady could see a number of other prints, some of them barefooted, leading into the strawberry patch where they disappeared.

"Could be it was Drover Hull," Brady suggested, "over here for the strawberries."

Range shook his head. "Not likely. There's several people been through here together, and when did you ever hear of Drover Hull traveling around with friends?"

Yet the footprints pointed in the direction of Drover Hull's place. Without a word Range and Brady set off together, walking quickly through the half mile of woods that lay between them and Drover Hull.

The farther they went, the more careful Range became. He seemed to listen with his whole body, Brady thought, dropping behind and letting Range lead the way. As far back as Brady could remember, Range had been a few steps ahead of him the way he was now, two years older and doing everything better than Brady could ever hope to. A person couldn't help but admire the way Range slipped among the shadows, his sights set steady on the glimmer of daylight ahead which meant they were coming out of the woods. Then as the daylight became stronger, Range crouched low. He darted from cover to cover, easing his way at last to some tall pokeweeds and broomstraw at the edge of the woods and motioning Brady over beside him. Bent almost double, the two boys slowly parted the weeds just enough to give them a view of the clearing.

There was the house, all right. A neat log cabin with a rocking chair set out by the door and a well beside it. There was the American flag that Drover Hull hung out in his front yard every fair day of the year, folks said. It struck Brady again how strange it was — this cabin and the American flag all alone, with the woods closing in on all sides — the same chestnuts, the same oaks that were here in the Indian days and even before that, maybe. It was hard to believe there was a town anywhere near with a bank, a store, a school and two churches, and a National Road not more than fifteen miles away that led all the way to Baltimore with stage-coaches every day and an express mail service.

There was no sign of Drover out in front. Brady changed his position slightly, as Range had already done, and parted the weeds in a different direction so that he could see the back of the house. At first Brady could hardly keep back a whistle of surprise. He nudged Range, but Range didn't move — just nodded and went on staring through his slit in the broomstraw. Brady looked again. Yes, it was true. Two colored men were working in Drover Hull's cornfield. Their backs were bare, their pants rolled up, and they were hoeing, turning the ground over around each young corn plant.

That wasn't the only surprise. Leaning up against the back of Drover Hull's cabin was Drover Hull himself and a third colored man, this one dressed respectably in city clothes. The two of them were stooped over a sheet of paper, and Drover's head with its wild shock of white hair going every which way was bobbing around as if he were excited about something. The other man began to walk back and forth as Drover talked, his head bent low. After a while he went over to the well and drew himself a drink. As he put the tin cup down from his face, all at once Brady saw who it was. It was Tar Adams, his father's barber, who had moved to town two years ago and kept a shop in the front room of the Jackson Hotel. *And he wasn't using his crutches.* As far as Brady knew, Tar Adams didn't take a step without those crutches. Brady himself had often watched the clever way Tar balanced on the crutches while he cut a man's hair and shaved him too. And here he was walking around free and easy as anyone!

Drover Hull, however, didn't seem surprised at Tar's walking. Drover was chewing tobacco, talking, and waving his arms about at the same time — such long, bony arms and his fingers were long too. Even from where Brady crouched he could see those long fingers crooked, spread apart, powerful. Could they, Brady wondered suddenly — *could they cure a cripple?* If Drover had really made Laban Williams sick that time, why couldn't he make Tar Adams well? All the witch stories that Brady had ever heard came flooding into his mind. Then Drover did a strange thing indeed. He took the paper he'd been looking at, tore it in half, leaned down and took off his shoes, and put half the paper in each shoe. As he straightened up, he spit. If it had been any other man, Brady wouldn't have thought a thing of that spit. Tobacco spit, he would have said. But coming from Drover, after that business with his shoes, Brady felt queer. Drover had seemed to look right into the woods and he had spit toward the very place where Brady and Range were hiding. Brady pulled his hands from his peephole in the weeds. Maybe that was the way Drover Hull cast his spells.

Brady poked Range. "Let's get out of here," he whispered.

This time he didn't wait for Range to lead the way. He just lit out and ran until his breath was pumped clear out of him; then he leaned up against a tree and while he waited for Range, he took stock of himself. He seemed to feel all right, he decided. If he was going to get a fever, like Laban Williams, at least he was pretty sure it hadn't started.

"Do you think Drover saw us?" Brady asked as Range caught up and they walked on together.

Range shook his head. "I know good and well he didn't. If you hadn't taken off like a bolt of lightnin', you'd have seen for yourself. Those men are still out there working in the fields."

"So? How does that figure?" Brady wished now he hadn't run so fast. He wished he had walked through the woods like Range, dipping his hand into the sack for a mouthful of berries now and then. Range was looking at him in a peculiar way.

"Don't you s'pose that Drover Hull would have had those men under cover pretty quick if he'd had an idea anyone was spying around?"

Brady had been so busy thinking about Drover and his spells, he hadn't taken time to think about the men. Why were they there anyway?

"You mean to say, Brady Minton," Range laughed, "that you haven't figured out who those men were?" Range popped some more berries into his mouth. "It's as plain as the nose on your face. Those men are runaway slaves and Drover Hull's place must be a station in the Underground Railroad."

Brady drew in his breath sharply. The Underground Railroad! Right here in Washington County, he said to himself. Of course in a town like Manna, that was only ten miles from the Virginia border, there was plenty of lively talk about slavery — some people, like Laban Williams' father, arguing that slavery was a good thing and others, like old Mr. McKain, taking the abolitionist stand and saying that slavery should be wiped out of the country tomorrow. Brady had seen slave catchers riding through, looking for runaways, but still slavery had seemed mostly talk and the Underground Railroad something you might read about in a book. The very name "Underground Railroad" suggested a fairy tale. When Brady had first heard the term, he had pictured a real underground train, but then, of course, it had been explained to him that the Underground Railroad referred to the routes taken by escaping slaves. The stations were the homes of northern friends where the runaways hid on the way.

"Which side are you on, Range?" Brady asked.

Range handed Brady some strawberries "Neither," he said. "It's not healthy to take sides. That's why I'm not going to tell anyone what we saw today and if you know what's good for you, you'll do the same."

The two boys separated to climb over some dead-wood piled across the path. "What about you?" Range asked as they came together. "Which side are you on?"

"Neither," Brady answered promptly.

"Didn't figure you could take sides, the way things are at your house — your ma from Virginia and your pa from the North," Range said. "Your ma and pa ever fight about it?"

Brady looked up through the trees and saw a black

crow circling in the sky. "Yes, they do," he said. He
pictured the way his mother's mouth tightened up at the
very mention of slavery. "Why don't you let Virginia
take care of her own business, Mr. Minton?" she would
say, talking as if there were company present. "I would
suppose you might find some wrongs right here in Pennsylvania to set about righting without traipsing all the
way over the border." Then she'd likely start talking
about Henry Clay and what he said and what he did.
And Brady's father would say Henry Clay never said
any such thing.

Why, just yesterday at the breakfast table the two of
them had got going again when suddenly Brady's father
had slammed his fist down on the table and stood up. "I
don't care whether Henry Clay says it's right or not or
what Calhoun says or anyone else!" he had shouted.
"What I care is what *God* says!" And he had slammed
out the back door. Through the open dining room
window Brady had watched him stride across the fields,
his shirttail flying, on the way to the Sermon House.

Range stopped and sat down on a flat rock to rest.
"Didn't see how they could help but have words now
and then," he said.

Brady looked up at the black crow. He kept his eye
on him circling dizzily over the trees, and then Brady
began to tell Range what had happened at the breakfast
table yesterday. He even told how his father had grown
so red in the face and how he'd slammed the door and
gone off with his shirttail flying. When he finished, he
looked at Range and he wished he hadn't told it. A little

smile was playing at the corners of Range's mouth and Brady knew that Range was trying to picture the Reverend Thaddeus Minton with his shirttail out, shouting at his wife.

Brady leaned down and picked up a stone and squeezed it until it hurt his hand and then he squeezed it some more. Why did he have to tell it? he asked himself. Why did he always have to tell everything?

Brady hunted for the crow. He had stopped his circling now and was streaking away over the trees, flapping and screeching, flapping and screeching. Brady would like to have taken the stone he held in his hand and flung it at that old crow, but then he noticed what Range was doing and instead he squeezed the stone harder than ever. Range had raised his rifle and was pointing it at the top of a hickory tree.

It seemed to Brady while he waited for Range to get ready, to level the gun, and to pull the trigger that he was holding his breath for the whole woods. Nothing is ever as hushed as the woods are the moment before a shot is fired. Not even the caw of the crow could be heard now.

Then the hush was shattered and the woods seemed to tremble and draw away from Brady as a squirrel fell limp at his feet. Range pushed the body over with his toes. "Aw, too bad," he said. "It's a female. Must have a new batch of young'uns in her nest. You can see she's been nursing."

Brady stood up and he could feel all the trees in the woods looking at him. Range was looking at him too.

Before he quite knew what he was doing, Brady started to climb the hickory tree.

"Where are you going?" Range asked.

Brady pulled himself up from branch to branch. He waited a moment to level his voice. "Just thought I'd take a look at the nest."

"Won't do you a bit of good," Range reminded him. "There's no way to save a nursing squirrel that's lost its ma. You know that, Brady."

Yes, he knew it all right. He didn't need any reminding, Brady told himself, edging his way over to the scraggly-looking nest in the fork of two branches.

Range stood at the foot of the tree, holding the dead squirrel, which Brady knew very well the Hadleys might or might not get around to skinning and eating. "How many are there?" Range called.

Brady looked into the nest at the four tiny bodies crawling over each other. "Four," he answered.

"Well, leave them alone," Range said. "Let's go. Don't worry about it, for land's sake. You know animals don't have the same feelings as folks do."

Brady let himself down to the ground. "Sure," he said. "I know."

Chapter Three

BRADY SET A FAST PACE going home. The woods were entirely too quiet now, an awful quiet broken only by the thin song of a silly bird who didn't know enough to keep still. "Weak," the bird sang. "Weak, weak." When the boys came to Miller's Creek, Brady was only too glad to leave the woods behind. He stopped at the

Hadleys' to pick up his trout and divide up the berries; then he hurried up the hill.

Matt would be home now, he told himself, driving his thoughts ahead, and the folks would be about ready to eat. Likely they were looking for him now. He stopped to shoo away a flock of red-winged blackbirds that had settled in the cornfields. He'd never seen the blackbirds as thick as they'd been the last few weeks. Generally they stayed in the swampy spots by the creek, but now there were so many, they were coming up the hill to see what food they could find.

Brady stopped out back at the pump to wash up. First he put his fish in a bucket of water to keep fresh. Then he brushed off the broomstraw that clung to his trousers, sponged the strawberry juice from the front of his shirt and pumped water over his dirty feet. He took the comb and the piece of broken looking glass that were lying beside the soap dish and he smoothed out his hair and flattened it down with water until it looked as good as Sunday. Now when he came in the kitchen, his grandmother would likely throw up her hands. "Pee-pul!" she would say. "Here's Brady, slicker'n a whistle." Brady even loosened his shirt collar and washed his neck.

When Brady walked into the kitchen, his grandmother and Aunt Sadie were busy at the stove and didn't turn around. His mother was dishing out applesauce into little bowls.

"Don't let the flies in, Brady," his mother said. "And go and wash up."

Brady set his poke of strawberries on the table and looked down at his clean bare feet. "I *am* washed up," he said.

His mother started to carry the dishes of applesauce into the dining room. "Well, clean up, then," she said briskly, brushing past him. "Put on a clean shirt and your Sunday trousers. And shoes, Brady."

"Sunday clothes!" Brady was shocked. "But we'll be going out to the barn and doing the chores right after supper."

"Then you can change back later," Mrs. Minton said. Her long skirts swished around the table as she set the applesauce down at each place.

For petey's sakes, Brady whispered to himself. "Where's Matt?" he asked.

"He must be either on the front porch with the men or in the back somewhere," Mrs. Minton said. "But don't look for him now. Clean up first."

When Brady walked into his bedroom and saw Matt's clothes laid out on the big double bed, his bags piled on the floor, and his books on the table, all at once he could hardly wait to see Matt. Oh, it was going to be good to have Matt home again, sharing the bedroom, poking him at night when he rolled over too far in bed. "Go on home, Brady," Matt always said. "Stay on your own side of the fence." Brady supposed things would be the same now with Matt. Surely becoming a professor wouldn't change a body too much.

Brady hurried into his good clothes, although, to tell the truth, he couldn't see what was good about them.

34

Stiff and unnatural, they seemed to him, struggling with
his collar in front of the open window. Then he caught
sight of Matt. He was way over beyond the side of the
house playing Anthony over-down, throwing a ball
over the apple tree to someone on the other side. He had
on his black Sunday trousers and a white shirt and somehow he seemed taller than Brady remembered. From
the back Matt looked just like his father; he even carried
his head slightly to one side the same way his father did.
Brady leaned out the window to see who was on the
other side of the tree. Uncle Will or Uncle Earl, most
likely. Instead, Mary Dorcas, her long golden curls flying behind her, was running for the ball.

Mrs. Minton came around to the back. "Mary
Dorcas!" she called.

Brady could see the pucker between his mother's eyes
that meant she was worried. Well, all the grown folks
seemed to worry about Mary Dorcas, not because she
was just getting over the measles either. They always
fretted over her as if she were made of thin teacup
china, for petey's sakes.

"Mary Dorcas," Mrs. Minton said, "you're going to
tucker yourself out running around like that so soon
after the measles."

Matt pulled one of Mary Dorcas' curls. "Guess you
better go in, young lady."

When Mary Dorcas and his mother had gone, Matt
leaned up against the house and looked over the hills.
Hanging out of the window above him, Brady knew
what Matt was thinking — glad to be home and feasting

his eyes on the countryside just as Brady himself had done earlier in the afternoon. Suddenly Brady grinned. He fished into his pocket and found a pebble he'd put in there sometime or other, and leaning out of the window again, he dropped it square on the top of Matt's head. He had to laugh to see Matt jump and look up at the window.

"Hey, Snapper!" Matt shouted. "*There* you are! What are you doing, boy?"

"Getting dressed for a company meal." With his head still out of the window, Brady smiled and slipped his necktie under his collar. "We're entertaining some fancy, stuck-up professor from Washington College."

"You don't say!" Matt laughed.

"A Professor Matthew Minton. Ma says you have to wear shoes when he comes."

Brady pulled his head in from the window and clattered down the stairs to join Matt at the dining room table.

"Well, how are things going?" Matt punched Brady in the ribs. "How's fishing?"

"First-rate. I caught a two-pounder today." Brady grinned.

"How's hunting?"

"Good." Brady kept right on grinning.

"Have you left any squirrels in the woods for me?"

Brady curled his toes up inside his tight shoes. "A few."

Then his father put an end to talk by saying grace,

and as Brady bowed his head, he gave himself up to enjoying the warm feeling that came over him whenever Matt was home. Everyone else must have been feeling the same way because as soon as the lids were lifted from the covered dishes, as soon as Mr. Minton had thrust his big pronged fork into the turkey, they all turned to Matt.

"Well, Professor," Uncle Will said. "Let's hear the news from Little Washington."

Brady watched Matt tuck the corner of his napkin into his vest and wondered what kind of story he'd brought home from Washington this time. The only thing Brady wished was that folks would stop calling the town where the college was *Little* Washington. It made the place sound second-rate while in reality it was not only a college town but the county seat as well. There was always something exciting going on there.

Last night there had been a street fight, Matt said. A traveling abolitionist preacher who called himself "Moses" Lowe had been attacked by a group of citizens with a bushel basket of eggs.

Well, that was what Brady meant. He couldn't remember ever having seen anything in Manna that you would call an out-and-out street fight. Folks could get worked up, all right, but never had Brady known anyone to throw an egg.

"Did the preacher get away?" Brady asked.

"Eventually. Some of Uncle Earl's deputies and the preacher's friends got him under cover, but even while he was being hustled away he was still declaiming that all slaves should be freed immediately, bloodshed or no bloodshed."

Mr. Minton shook his head. "The abolitionists are doing more harm than good talking about immediate freedom. If only they'd be patient and work for gradual emancipation, they'd serve our cause a lot better."

"And make it easier for me," Uncle Earl agreed. "As long as I'm sheriff, I'll do my best to protect them, but if traveling preachers are going to sound off unexpectedly, I'll need a lot more deputies. Why, this man goes around telling folks he's Moses, come back to lead the slaves to their freedom."

"Did you hear how your deputies made out last night, Earl?" Uncle Will asked.

"They managed to arrest a few of the egg throwers."

Mrs. Minton had been holding the big crockery milk pitcher, ready to pour from it. Instead she set it down hard on the table. "Well, I never!" Her eyes were snapping. "Arresting the egg throwers! It was that preacher they should have arrested, Earl Minton!"

Brady was inclined to agree with his mother; then his father started talking and Brady wasn't sure what he thought. How could a person make up his mind in a house like this, for petey's sakes? Now Mr. Minton was saying that, of course, the traveling preacher had a right to say what he pleased even if he did use poor judgment and had queer notions. Everybody had that right. The rest of the family joined in, saying that the country would be in a poor way, indeed, without free speech.

On and on. Everyone seemed to have something to say except Mary Dorcas, of course, and Brady.

Brady cleaned up his plate, then looked out the window and counted six red-winged blackbirds on the grass. More were coming up from the hollow. All at once Brady realized that he had something important to say too. He wondered why he hadn't thought of it before. He had a piece of slavery news that would make everyone sit up and take notice.

"You'll never guess what I saw today," he said.

At first no one seemed to hear. His mother was standing up with the empty gravy bowl that needed refilling. She looked as if she'd heard enough about free speech. "I still say there ought to be a law," she said, turning to the kitchen. "No preacher or anyone else ought to be allowed to say things aimed to rile folks and set one part of the country against another." As soon as she'd spoken, she went into the kitchen.

"You'll never guess what I saw today," Brady repeated. He looked around the long table and waited for the family, one by one, to become interested. Matt and Mary Dorcas looked at Brady. Then Brady's grandmother, his Aunt Sadie, Uncle Earl, and Uncle Will. Mrs. Minton came back and sat down at the table. At last Mr. Minton looked up too.

"A wildcat," Mr. Minton suggested.

Brady shook his head. The folks would surely be surprised, he thought. His story was every bit as interesting as Matt's, if not more so.

"I bet it was a peddler," Brady's grandmother said,

her eyes twinkling. "He had something in his knapsack that took your eye."

"No."

"An eagle," Mary Dorcas suggested.

"Nope." Brady grinned. "It was an Underground Railroad station. I saw it with my own eyes. Over by Drover Hull's. He's the agent and he's got two runaways over there."

Brady talked fast, but before he'd finished he knew that something had gone wrong. The room was quiet in the same awful way that the woods had been quiet after Range shot the squirrel. No one said a word. Mr. Minton put his knife and fork down on his plate, crossing them like the letter X. Then he leaned across the table the way he did sometimes in the pulpit and his face looked as if it were Judgment Day.

"You are mistaken, Brady," he said. "You imagine things and I don't want to hear another word about it now or ever. I forbid you to spread such tales elsewhere. Moreover, I forbid you to go to that cabin again."

Then everyone started to talk all at once about everything under the sun except the Underground Railroad. It was as if Brady hadn't spoken at all or as if he had said something embarrassing or, worse still, as if he had told a falsehood, which was apparently what his father thought.

"But I'm telling you —" Brady started to protest when he felt Matt's foot come down hard on top of his own.

It was Aunt Sadie who filled the gap in the conversation this time. "Oh dear," she sighed, "just look at Mary Dorcas' plate. She's hardly eaten a thing."

Everybody looked at Mary Dorcas and her plate and said no wonder she was so peaked, she didn't eat enough to keep a bird alive, and didn't she know that carrots put roses in your cheeks?

Uncle Will turned to Brady's mother. "How does it feel to have a girl in the family after all your boys?"

Mrs. Minton beamed. "Oh, it feels wonderful," she said. "I always wanted a girl, you know."

After that, the folks seemed to forget the awful quiet but Brady didn't. He still didn't know what he had done and he felt uncomfortable through the rest of the meal. Right up until the time Mr. Minton pushed back his chair. He asked Brady to bring the pen and ink and the Family Bible to the table.

Then Brady put the incident out of his mind. His father was going to write in the Bible. You couldn't go on worrying at a time like this. Brady handed his father the Bible and watched him undo the brass clasps and open the leather covers. Then he turned to the pages marked FAMILY HISTORY at the back of the book, and Brady felt the thrill of excitement that always came when a new notation was to be added. He looked over his father's shoulder at the faded handwriting of his great-grandfather Hugh at the top of the first page. Brady could barely make out the first entry dated 1765. *On this day*, his great-grandfather had written, *I landed in America*. Next in the history came his grandfather's small, precise writing and now his father's. Brady could count on his fingers the number of times he'd watched his father write in the Bible, and although the entries were never about him, still he felt as if he had participated in the importance of each moment, as if the whole family had somehow moved on a notch in the making of its history. There was the record of Luke's marriage and of Aunt Nell's death. Before that was the time that Luke had rescued the Post children from their burning house and the time, May 28, 1825, when Matt had shaken hands with General Lafayette. Brady's father always said there were other times besides deaths and births that were important to a family, although up to now Brady's birth was the only thing about him that had been worth putting down.

Mr. Minton dipped his pen in the ink. *June 10, 1836. On this day, Matthias Minton was officially installed Professor of History at Washington College.*

Mr. Minton passed the Bible around the table for everyone to see and when it came back to him, he opened it in the middle, read aloud the one hundredth Psalm and led the family in prayer. Afterwards, each member of the family, as he left the table, congratulated Matt again.

You would have thought that a fellow who was receiving that much attention wouldn't bother to help with the evening chores, but when Brady went upstairs to change into his old clothes, Matt went along and changed too.

Being a professor hadn't spoiled Matt a bit. Later as

they were getting ready for bed, Brady thought happily that everything seemed just the same as it had before. Matt was sitting on the bed untying his shoes. He had a way of sticking the tip of his tongue out of the corner of his mouth when he was struggling with something, whether it was a knot in a shoelace or a difficult idea, and Brady smiled now to see the tip of Matt's tongue as he bent over. But it wasn't the shoelace, after all, that was giving Matt trouble.

"Brady," Matt said. The way he spoke, Brady knew that Matt had something on his mind. "Do you know why I stepped on your foot tonight?"

Brady walked over to the window and looked out. A cluster of three stars hovered over the barn roof. "No."

"Don't you know what you said?"

"Sure I know what I said. It was true, too."

One of Matt's shoes dropped on the floor.

"Do you think it was something to repeat?" Matt asked. "Uncle Earl, a sheriff, was sitting right across the table from you. If he doesn't know about runaways, he doesn't have to do anything about them. It's not a job a man with his sympathies cares for — helping to send a runaway back South. The less he knows about the Underground Railroad, the happier he is."

Standing by the window, Brady could feel his face growing hot. He'd done it again. Talked out of turn.

"What you saw is the kind of thing a man doesn't talk about," Matt went on. "That kind of news could get a heap of people in trouble. Suppose Laban Williams' father and that crowd got wind of a thing like that? The Underground Railroad is nothing to fool with, Brady. *It's a matter of life and death*."

Brady gripped the edge of the window sill as he heard Matt moving around behind him, putting his clothes away.

"Top drawer still mine?" Matt asked.

Brady nodded.

"You know in Washington there was an agent that was caught," Matt said. "It came out at the time that man had as many as ten slaves concealed in his barn for a couple of weeks or more, waiting for word from the next station saying it was safe to send them on. All that time that man fed those runaways and *not one person in his family knew a thing about it*. When you know that kind of news, Brady, you don't tell *anyone*."

Slowly and miserably Brady turned around and faced Matt. How could you tell a brother who was a professor and had just been written down in the Bible that you wished you could cut your tongue out? But Brady didn't need to say anything. Matt seemed to know. He smiled and picked up a pillow from the bed and threw it at Brady.

"Had any pillow fights lately, Snapper?" he asked.

Brady flung the pillow back at Matt. In a minute they were using both pillows and Matt was standing on the bed, defending the ramparts, just as he had done years ago before he went to college and when Luke was still home.

Flushed and out of breath, Brady stopped for a minute. "You're going to stay home for the summer, aren't you, Matt? You won't start teaching before fall, will you?"

Matt held back the pillows. "I'll be here for a week," he said. "Then I have to go back. I'm filling out another man's term and I'll be teaching right through the summer session. Why don't you come and visit me soon? Seems to me you're old enough to ride over to Washington by yourself."

Brady's shoulders sagged. "Huh!" he grunted. "You tell Pa that. Likely I'll be voting before he trusts me to go to Washington alone."

"I'll speak to Pa," Matt promised. "Maybe by the end of summer he'll let you come." Matt threw the pillows at Brady, one after the other.

Later when the two brothers went to bed, Brady found that he was too stirred up to fall asleep. He lay on his back and stared at the ceiling while all the events of the day turned into pictures and moved back and forth before him, refusing to be put to rest. The picture of his father telling him he was mistaken about the Underground Railroad kept coming back in spite of all he could do, and the picture of Tar Adams walking without his crutches, and of Drover Hull spitting into the woods. Then as he felt himself almost at the border line of sleep, Brady saw a scraggly nest in the fork of a tree and four small bodies wriggling around in it.

At last Brady got up and went to the window. The sky was spotted with stars now and in the distance were the woods, standing tall and black at the foot of the hjll. Maybe if he filled his eyes with real sights he could forget the pictures that kept coming into bed with him, but it didn't work that way. When Brady looked at the woods, all he could see was that scraggly old nest. And what he heard made him feel worse than ever. From out of the barn, Catfish walked into the night, crying and looking into the shadows and crying again.

All at once Brady had an idea. He didn't know whether it would work, but it was worth trying. He would get up in the morning before anyone else was awake and see what would happen.

This time when Brady went to bed, it didn't take him long to fall asleep. He was just dropping off when he felt Matt poke him. "Go on home, Brady," Matt mumbled sleepily. "Stay on your own side of the fence."

Chapter Four

B RADY HAD A WAY of setting his mind for a certain
hour when he went to bed and waking up at that
time in the morning. He was pretty accurate, too —
more so than the clock they had bought from his father's
friend, Mr. Parley Potter, the traveling clockman, who
had to fix it every time he came through.

It was barely light when Brady went out. The sky

had a faint pink glow at one side and a lingering star at the other. As he walked across the top of the hill, leaving the sleeping household behind, Brady had the feeling he always had at this time of day — as if at any moment he might come across a secret not meant for the rest of the world. He peered in the window of the Sermon House as he passed and tried the door, but it was closed tight as a tinderbox.

Brady chose the most direct path into the woods, steering clear of the Hadleys. The last thing he wanted was to meet anyone and have to answer a lot of questions before he knew for certain if his idea would work out.

He didn't have far to go. He remembered exactly where it was — the flat rock he'd been sitting on and the hickory tree across from it. As Brady climbed the tree, he decided that the best thing to do would be to take the whole nest. He smiled when he looked into the nest. They were there, all right — all four of them and mighty hungry too from all appearances. He worked the nest loose from the fork of the branches and, holding it next to his body with one hand, he eased his way down the tree with his other.

He started right home, holding the nest so he could look into it as he walked. One of the squirrels seemed to be much smaller than the other three, he noticed. He didn't know why but the smallest one in any litter of animals usually seemed to be the one that he liked best. Maybe it would be so this time too. He took the smallest squirrel out and held it in the palm of his hand, but after a moment he put it back. "What am I thinking of?" he said crossly to himself. "I don't even know if it's going to work."

He was paying so much attention to the squirrels that he had passed the Sermon House and was almost to the barn before he saw Mary Dorcas. She was sitting on the grass, doing nothing, just looking into space, for petey's sakes.

Brady tried to hide the nest behind his back. "What are you doing here this time of day?" he snapped.

Mary Dorcas jumped to her feet. "Just looking around." She hesitated and pushed back her curls which didn't look rightly combed yet.

"I like to be the first one up and kind of watch the world come to life," she said. "Do you too?"

"Do I too — what?" Brady growled, deliberately misunderstanding her and turning himself around in a circle as she tried to walk behind him.

"What have you got?" Mary Dorcas asked. "A bird's nest?"

A bird's nest! That's all she knew. Without thinking, Brady brought the nest around and showed her.

"I suppose you think those are birds in there, too," he said. Then for a moment, as he saw her face fire up, he was almost sorry he'd spoken so sharply. "Their mother was killed," he explained gruffly, "and if you want to know what I'm going to do, you can come in and watch me. Only if you do, you'll have to be quiet."

Brady didn't really expect Mary Dorcas to be quiet. From his experience, he'd learned that girls squeal the way dogs bark and there's not much you can do about it. But when they went into the kitchen, Mary Dorcas sat down on the round three-legged stool and didn't say a word while Brady lifted the squirrels out gently one at a time and put them in Catfish's box behind the kitchen stove. Then he went outside and found Catfish sleeping under the back steps and carried her into the box with the squirrels.

Catfish didn't have her feet down flat before she realized there was something going on. She put her nose down and sniffed the squirrels, going from one to another. Then she began from the beginning and sniffed them again, her tail jerking up and down in stiff, excited jerks. It was as if she were counting and saying to herself, "How did this happen? I lost two kittens and now I have four."

At least that was what Brady hoped Catfish was thinking. She might, of course, be deciding that these were strange animals, indeed, and she wouldn't have a thing to do with them. While Brady held his breath, Catfish turned around and around in the box, and then she flopped down and made room for the four squirrels to have their breakfast.

"Look at that," Brady whispered. He moved the smallest squirrel close to Catfish to make sure it wouldn't miss out.

Mary Dorcas crept softly behind the stove and bent over the box to watch. The only sound in the kitchen was a deep, rumbling mother-cat purr. It was what Brady's grandmother heard a few minutes later when she stopped in the kitchen doorway to tie her apron-strings.

"What on earth?" she said, talking out loud to herself as she often did. From where she was standing, she couldn't see Mary Dorcas or Brady. "Sounds like a sawmill."

Brady's grandmother was so large that she filled the doorway and it took her longer than most women to tie an apron. "Couldn't be Catfish, could it? Over her mourning already?" Then she came over behind the stove.

"Pee-*pul!*" she exclaimed.

One by one, as the household assembled, they listened to Brady's story and stood smiling around Catfish's box.

"Never did I see the like," Aunt Sadie said when the women had done looking and set about making breakfast.

Brady looked up from the box and grinned at Matt who had stayed to marvel some more. It occurred to Brady, then, that someone was missing.

"Where's Pa?" he asked.

"You better fetch him, Brady." Mrs. Minton was mixing a bowl of hot-cake batter. "Your father got up while it was still dark and went down to his Sermon House," she explained. "He must have had an idea in the night and thought it couldn't wait. You know how he is."

Brady knew, all right. Sometimes in the middle of plowing a field, his father would take off for the Sermon House, saying he had a thought he had to get down on paper while it was still fresh in his mind. Since today was Saturday, he would likely spend most of his time there, getting ready for the Sabbath. His mother wouldn't be disturbing Pa now, except that Uncle Will and Aunt Sadie and Grandma were leaving for home right after breakfast and he would be wanting to say good-by. And there was no sense ringing the dinner bell for Pa — not while he was in the Sermon House. In the first place, he likely wouldn't hear it, and if he did, he'd figure it might be for someone else and wouldn't waste his time to find out.

"Just keep knocking on the door, Brady, until he comes," Mrs. Minton said.

"And don't go busting in," Matt added while everybody laughed. "Have you ever been in his Sermon House, Ma?" Matt asked.

"*Me?* Don't be simple." Mrs. Minton's eyes were twinkling. "He's afraid I might disturb something with my dustcloth."

Brady smiled at his mother's words as he went out to fetch his pa. He recalled that his pa always said he'd been chased out of his own house by folks running back and forth borrowing things, washing windows and asking the time of day, and he didn't want his family poking around, making themselves at home in his new quarters.

Brady knocked at the door of the Sermon House and tried to picture his father inside at his desk, frowning at the interruption and calling out, "Who is it?" He would open the door then, and come out so quickly that there would be no chance to get even a peek into the dark room behind him.

Brady knocked again but there was no answer. Deciding that his father must be asleep, he knocked louder and called out to his father, but there was no rousing him. Brady was about to go around to the side and rap at a window when he saw that his father was not in the Sermon House at all. He was coming up the hill from the direction of the woods, walking slowly with his head lowered as if he were very tired.

"Thought I'd look around and check some of our fences," Mr. Minton explained as he joined Brady and they walked to the house together.

Well, that was a strange thing for his father to do so early on a Saturday morning, Brady thought. Then he looked down at his father's trousers.

"Why, Pa," he said in surprise, "you're covered with broomstraw."

Mr. Minton stopped and brushed off his trousers. "So I am," he said shortly.

This was queer too. Brady sent his mind racing over the Minton property because, as far as he could recall, there wasn't any broomstraw there. He opened his mouth to ask his father just where he had been, but Mr. Minton didn't give him a chance to say anything.

"I've been noticing, Brady," Mr. Minton said, "that the place is overrun with blackbirds. They don't do much harm now but they may when the corn is farther along. I want you to make a scarecrow and get it up as soon as you can."

This was a job Brady liked. He forgot about the broomstraw as he began planning just how he wanted the scarecrow to be. "I'll make a good one," he promised. "There won't be a blackbird dare come near, it'll be so real-looking."

"Well, don't make it so lifelike," Mr. Minton said dryly, "that it will start to talk. We have enough of that around here as it is."

Brady followed slowly. His infernal habit of talking out of turn seemed to stick up in his father's mind like one of those big oak stumps in the pasture, its roots so stubborn it took you an age and a day to pry it loose. Why did his father have to think about that now, anyway?

As it happened, Brady didn't have a chance to work on the scarecrow for several days. On Saturdays the folks were always busy getting ready for the Sabbath. Mrs. Minton would spend most of the time in the kitchen, cooking ahead for the next day, and Brady and his Uncle Earl would clean up the week's work outside. On the Sabbath, of course, no one would work at all. You spent most of that day in church sitting and listening and halfway hoping that a horse would break loose outside or something happen to release you. So, what with one thing and another, it was the middle of the next week before Brady gathered his materials together and sat down outside under the dining room window to start work on his scarecrow.

His mother had let him have a piece of white cloth

he was going to stuff with straw for the head, an old
shirt of his father's, and that raggedy long-tailed jacket
she had made out of some old black cotton years ago
for Luke to wear at a school recitation when he had
dressed up as Uncle Sam. Brady grinned as he hammered two strips of board together to form the frame.
His scarecrow was going to be a comical-looking fellow, all right.

Mary Dorcas and his mother were sitting inside by
the open dining room window. His mother was quilt-
ing; Mary Dorcas was knitting on a pair of white socks
which she put aside every once in a while to poke her
head out of the window and ask Brady how he was
coming.

"What are you going to use for a hat, Brady?" Mary
Dorcas asked.

Well, to tell the truth, that was troubling Brady
some; there didn't seem to be an old hat anywhere
around. "I suppose he'll just have to go bareheaded,"
Brady said.

"But he'll look so bald," Mary Dorcas complained.
"You ought at least to give him some hair."

She withdrew from the window but a minute later
she popped her head back.

"I'm going to make your scarecrow a wig," she said.
"Auntie says I may."

She disappeared again and Brady could hear her talking and planning with his mother.

It was peaceful under the dining room window. Bees
were buzzing in and out of the cabbage roses on one side

of Brady. Catfish and her family of squirrels were in
their box on the other side. The squirrels were getting
along fine. The biggest ones were crawling in and out
of the box so much now that they had to be taken out
of the kitchen. It was a sight to see them running about
and Catfish following with a puzzled air. Brady walked
over and took the smallest squirrel out of the box.

"Come on out, Skinny," he said, "and see what the
world looks like."

As he sat down again, Brady glanced in the window.
Mary Dorcas was doing something with a bunch of
white yarn and she had that rapt expression on her face
which meant she was listening again to his mother tell
about when she was a little girl in Virginia. Mrs. Minton didn't talk much about her home any more, the way
she used to when Brady was little. Only to Mary
Dorcas, who never tired of hearing the stories. Brady,
too, had to admit it gave him pleasure to hear them
again. It seemed to him now, listening to the murmur
of his mother's voice, that he could almost see his
mother's old home, its eucalyptus trees, its rolling lawns
stretched out in front of him. He could see his mother
and her colored mammy, Auntie Lil, sitting under that
big magnolia she talked about, making doll clothes or
shelling peas or whatever. The way his mother talked
about her home, it seemed hard to believe that it was
part of the same South that old Mr. McKain ranted
against. And you could scarcely credit the fact that
Auntie Lil was a slave.

Brady had got as far as attaching the stuffed head of

his scarecrow to the body when all at once his mother's voice stopped in the middle of a sentence. Brady could hear knocking at the front door, his mother's quick footsteps, and then from outside somewhere, his father's big welcoming voice.

In a moment his father came around the corner of the house with Mr. Parley Potter, of all people, the traveling clockman who was supposed to have gone to his home in Virginia to stay for the summer. Mr. Potter was a fat, amiable gentleman who talked as if he had been wound up like one of his clocks. His favorite subject was mental arithmetic, and he never came but what he spieled off figures for Brady to work in his head. Full of jokes, still he was one of those grownups who always managed, it seemed to Brady, to make you feel uncomfortable.

"Brady, my boy!" he boomed as Brady stood up to greet him. "Great day in the morning! Look how that boy has grown. Most big enough now to go out sparkin' the girls! What you eatin', boy, that stretches you out so? Give me the recipe and I'll sell it instead of clocks." The gold watch chain across Mr. Potter's flowered waistcoat jiggled up and down and the glass buttons on his jacket twinkled in the sunshine.

"How are your numbers today, boy? You're keeping on your toes, I hope." He folded his arms across his waistcoat and teetered back and forth like a pendulum in slow motion. "Let's see what you can do with this. Five hundred and forty-two plus six hundred and forty-five."

Five and two are seven, Brady figured, but as usual he never had time to complete the answer. Mr. Potter was snapping his fingers. "Faster, faster," he said. "Quick on the trigger, that's the ticket to success. And some day you'll wind up President, eh, Mr. Minton?" He jabbed Brady's father in the ribs, then turned away, not waiting for the numbers that were so slow in coming.

Brady picked up his scarecrow. One thousand, one hundred and eighty-seven, he muttered to himself. He fitted the shirt on the scarecrow and then the long-tailed jacket. Mary Dorcas came out and fastened on the wig of white yarn that she'd made. It looked so good that Brady grinned and forgot about Mr. Potter and his figures. "I reckon a blackbird will think twice before he comes near this scarecrow," Brady said.

"You're going to put a face on him, aren't you?" Mary Dorcas asked. "I brought you a piece of old charcoal so you could."

Brady drew two round circles for eyes and a long line for the nose, but when he came to the mouth, he stopped and handed Mary Dorcas her piece of charcoal.

"He doesn't need a mouth," Brady explained shortly. "He's got no cause to talk."

Then with Mary Dorcas running ahead, Brady took his scarecrow and planted it right in the middle of the cornfield. As he stepped back to admire it, he looked across the fields and caught sight of his father and Mr. Potter.

"For petey's sakes," Brady muttered.

His father was taking Mr. Parley Potter into the Sermon House. His arm was around Mr. Potter's shoulders as they went through the door. And the door closed behind them.

Just wait until I tell the folks *that*, Brady thought. He looked back at the scarecrow with its big staring eyes and the blank place where its mouth should have been. Brady pressed his lips together. Maybe he'd tell and maybe he wouldn't.

Then as he kept looking at the scarecrow standing there, so lonely above the young corn plants, its long, thin, black arms stretched out and pointing, its patch of white hair blowing wildly in the breeze, Brady had the strangest feeling crawl up his spine. He hadn't set out to do it, but he'd made his scarecrow look exactly like Drover Hull.

Chapter Five

Brady couldn't look at his scarecrow without being reminded of Drover Hull. At first, after he'd made the awful mistake of telling the folks he'd discovered an Underground Railroad station, Brady thought he'd steer clear of the whole business. He didn't want to see Drover Hull again and he didn't care what happened to the runaways, but as the days went by, Brady decided it wasn't necessary to take such a strong stand. It would be foolish to deny himself the pleasure of walking through the woods and if he saw anything going on at Drover Hull's place, he would know enough this time to keep quiet about it. Matt had gone back to Washington and for the past several days there had been nothing but work and more work. Brady figured that the first chance he got, he'd slip down to Range's and propose a trip into the woods. When you knew there was an Underground Railroad station so close, it kind of nagged at you.

Before Brady could get away, however, Range came up to the Mintons' and asked Brady to go into town with him. He had to stop at the post office for his pa, Range said, and pick up a length of wire at the store. Mrs. Minton gave Brady a few errands to do and two pennies to spend on candy. Then, as he was leaving the house, Brady glanced at the clock on the mantelpiece and he felt provoked all over again. It didn't keep time at all and Mr. Parley Potter had come and gone without touching it. He had paraded his flowered waistcoat all over the Minton property and talked mental arithmetic, then left without attending to the one piece of business that was rightfully his.

"You know what I wish your pa would do?" Brady grumbled as he and Range walked toward town together. "I wish he'd invent a clock that didn't need fixing every few days."

But Range wasn't thinking about his pa nor about clocks either.

"I heard a piece of news the other day," he said slowly, squinting at the sun, "that might interest your folks. Bill Williams, Laban's pa, says he's sick and tired of the abolitionists in the county stirring up trouble. He's organized a group of men that aim to stop it."

Brady shrugged. "My father's no abolitionist. Nor my Uncle Earl either. They may be against slavery but they never joined up with any wild abolitionist outfit like Mr. McKain did."

Range jingled the few coins he had in his pocket. "Mr. Williams and his cronies say if the sheriff can't keep the abolitionists quiet and if he can't discourage runaway slaves, it's time someone else did. When the next election comes around, they say they're going to put a man in the sheriff's office who shows more interest in keeping the peace."

So that was it. Brady scuffed his feet into the straight path a wagon wheel had made. He thought how hard Uncle Earl worked, helping Brady's father on the farm when he could, riding all over the county on his sheriff's business, staying overnight in Washington whenever court was in session and other times too. Since the street fight in Washington, he'd hardly been home at all. What was Mr. Williams talking about anyway? Uncle Earl had a fine record.

"That ain't all either," Range said. "Young Laban came skulkin' around our place the other day, pretending to be lookin' for runaways. He didn't go into the woods, I noticed. Just bragged a lot. But I guess if there's goin' to be trouble, he'll help make it."

Brady broke off a long green shoot growing at the side of the road. He switched it in front of him, then snapped off the head of a daisy. What a sneaky, low-down, bigmouthed, good-for-nothing Laban Williams was! All the way down one hill and past Post's deserted mill, Brady and Range talked about Laban, naming the mean things he'd done at one time or another. They might have gone on talking about him until they reached town, but old Mr. McKain lived at the bottom of the last hill and he put a stop to all talk but his own. There was nothing Mr. McKain liked better than to waylay a passer-by and get his ear.

He was sitting in a chair beside his house with a rifle across his knees. In the front yard Brady could see the cannon Mr. McKain had brought home with him from the War of Independence. He'd shot it off once or twice since the war in honor of some important event and folks said he still had a good supply of cannon balls in his cellar. All Brady hoped was that he'd be around when Mr. McKain saw fit to fire his cannon again. Right now he was giving his rifle a workout. Every once in a while as Brady and Range approached, Mr. McKain took a shot at a red-winged blackbird.

"There you go," he shouted each time a blackbird fell. "Now bring on your reinforcements! Advance and be killed, you dirty English redcoats!"

Range grinned. "He's off again," he said. "Fightin' the Battle of Yorktown. Let's try and slip by without his seeing us."

Brady nodded. Once Mr. McKain cornered you, he'd

either tell you about the campaigns he'd fought in the War of Independence or else he'd get going on slavery. There was no stopping him either way.

Brady and Range went to the far side of the road and stepped in among the shadows of the trees, but they weren't quick enough. A person would have to get up early in the morning before he could fool Mr. McKain.

"Mornin', boys," he called and he didn't even appear to look at them. His eyes were following a blackbird and his gun was raised. "Nice day, ain't it?" He pulled the trigger.

Reluctantly the two boys crossed the road. Mr. McKain was wearing his old campaign hat and under the brim, his eyes were sparkling as he surveyed the ground in front of him littered with the bodies of dead birds. He swept his hand before him.

"This ain't nothin'," he said, "compared to what we done to the passenger pigeons. That was long before your time. Pigeons would come over in such swarms, you couldn't even see the sun. You'd fire one shot and, by jingo, you'd bring down a whole platoon." Mr. McKain chuckled. "When we were done, there were such hills of dead pigeons we'd have to dig them under and that's a fact. You don't hardly see a pigeon any more."

Brady looked at the dead birds strewn on the ground. They were pretty things — shiny black with a little patch of red high on each wing like a soldier's decoration. Of course Brady knew a farmer had to protect his crops; still he couldn't help but feel sorry about the blackbirds and the pigeons too.

"Do you suppose we have to shoot them all?" he ventured.

Mr. McKain waved his rifle as if it were a flag. "Why not?" he shouted. "Why in blazes not? If the Lord had meant there to be more blackbirds than people, He would have given them shotguns instead of us."

He turned to Brady. "What's your pa doin' about them?" he asked.

"Well, we have a scarecrow up in the cornfield. It's doing some good," Brady said.

Mr. McKain stood up. He pulled his cap down and studied the sky. "That ain't enough," he said. "We never will get rid of the pesky things unless we band together." He threw back his head. "Why, if folks didn't know enough to band together," he shouted, "we'd still be swearin' allegiance to the king. I mind the time — "

Range winked at Brady. "We have to be on our way, Mr. McKain," he interrupted. "We have some errands to do."

As they walked away, Brady grinned. Range was slippery as an eel. If Brady had been alone, he'd likely be there for the next hour, standing first on one foot and then on the other.

They had only one more hill to go down now. Looking at the town of Manna from here — and the little houses clustered together — Brady guessed this must be the prettiest town in Pennsylvania, even if there wasn't much happening in it. Maybe it was the prettiest in the whole country, he said to himself a few minutes later as he walked down the main street. The houses beneath their shade trees opened their front porches wide and sent little paths running down to meet you. Honeysuckle clung to porch railings and peeked in kitchen windows. Children in front yards and old men in rocking chairs called out to Brady and Range as they passed.

The boys went to the post office first and then to the store where they completed their errands and Brady bought a banana candy apiece.

"There's no need to hurry right home, I guess," Brady observed. "Maybe we can find some excitement if we look hard enough."

"Maybe," Range said and they stopped to look in the open door of the blacksmith shop.

The Jackson Hotel was the next building up the street. Brady glanced in the window of the barbershop. He had almost forgotten about Tar Adams, but there he was just as usual, cutting a man's hair, acting no different than he ever did. His crutches were under the pits of his arms and you could see him leaning the weight of his body on them while he snipped his scissors up and down, back and forth.

Brady nudged Range. "Look at that," he whispered. "His legs have got bad again."

Now Tar was brushing off the man in the chair, then walking with him to the door. He was swinging along between his crutches, his legs dangling uselessly. Drover's spell, if it had been a spell, had certainly worn off.

Tar came outside and lowered himself onto the stool he kept there so he could sit in the sun between customers.

"There," he sighed. "Feels good to let the old bones down." He handed Brady his crutches. "Lean those beside me, son, while I get out my tobacco."

Brady took the crutches, but before he put them down, he slipped them under his arms. What was it like to be a cripple? he wondered. "Can I try them, Tar?" he asked.

Tar was shaking tobacco into his hand. "Go ahead, boy. Help yourself."

The crutches were so long that Brady had to spread them apart and leap into the air in order to make any progress at all. Pretending that his bones ached the way Tar's did, he proceeded slowly up the street, his eyes on the ground. Now he tried to see how far he could go on each new leap. He would make a mark on the dirt road with the tip of a crutch, then swing himself forward and look back to gauge the distance. Two feet. Three feet. It was too bad there wasn't another pair of crutches around so he and Range could have a race. Three and a half feet. The clump of the crutches and his own feet landing were the only sounds he could hear. And then Brady saw the stranger. Or rather, because he was still concentrating so hard on the ground, Brady saw the dog. A bloodhound with watery red eyes and a loose drooling lower lip. No one in Manna owned a bloodhound. You didn't have that kind of dog unless you had a special job for it to do. Brady looked up and the first thing he saw was the jagged red scar that ran up the left side of the stranger's face and into his eye. You wouldn't forget a face like that even if you didn't suspect it belonged to a slave catcher.

"Hello, sonny," the stranger said. "I'll bet those crutches aren't yours." The man was smiling and his voice was pleasant enough; still, Brady found himself tucking the crutches quickly under one arm and turning back toward the hotel.

"No, sir," he replied shortly.

The stranger fell into step beside him. "Didn't think so," he said. "When I saw you coming up the street, I said to my dog, Snake, 'Now here comes a likely-looking boy with nothing better to do than play with a pair of crutches. Maybe he'd like to earn some easy money.'" The man reached into his pocket and pulled out a silver coin and tossed it lightly into the air. "I'm looking for runaway slaves," he said. He winked at Brady and the two ends of his scar jackknifed together. "Thought you might have seen or heard of some in these parts."

"No. Never heard of any." Brady quickened his pace.

"Well, you might know of some likely hiding places. An abolitionist barn, a deserted mill. Maybe an out-of-the-way woods a person wouldn't see from the road. You look like the sort of boy who wouldn't miss much that goes on."

By this time they were almost to the hotel. Brady could see Range and a group of five or six men loafing by the entrance, talking to Tar on his camp stool. The slave catcher saw Tar too.

"Who's the darkie?" he asked.

"Tar Adams. He's a freedman. He's got a barbershop in town."

"Been here long?"

"A couple of years."

"Hm." The slave catcher stepped in front of Brady and walked directly to Tar Adams.

"Nice mornin'," he said. He rocked slowly back and forth on his feet as if he were waiting for Tar to jump up and pay his respects, but Tar didn't move. The bloodhound sniffed at Tar's feet but Tar didn't even look at him.

"I thought maybe I could strike a bargain with you. That is," the slave catcher paused pointedly, "if you *are* a sure-enough freedman."

There was something about the slave catcher's voice that made the men standing around move in closer. All at once then Brady remembered about slave catchers and free Negroes. A slave catcher was supposed to like nothing better than to happen on a free Negro, figuring a Negro would know more than any white man about runaways and could be badgered into telling what he knew. And if he didn't tell, that free Negro might suddenly find himself on the southern side of the border being sold as a slave again. At least that had happened more than once.

And now look what he'd done, Brady thought. He'd

led the slave catcher straight to Tar Adams and the slave catcher was getting mad. His scar was jerking up and down angrily.

"Generally when I strike a bargain with a man," he said, biting off his words sharp, "that man is standing up."

It seemed to Brady he'd never seen Tar act so slow. He scratched his head, lazy as a cat, and nodded to a couple of men who were joining the group. Then he reached his hand over to Brady for his crutches and pulled himself slowly upright.

"I don't rightly know what kind of bargain you could strike with an old cripple like me," he said.

Brady watched the slave catcher's scar turn red as he looked at the crutches and realized for the first time they belonged to Tar. The men began to snicker and pass jokes back and forth. Brady hadn't thought of it, but, after all, being a cripple made Tar pretty safe. You couldn't sell a cripple as a slave nor expect much help from one. Brady wondered what the slave catcher would do now. He looked mad and mean enough to start a street fight, but instead he just kicked out at his dog and muttered something ugly under his breath. If he had it in mind to do anything more, he didn't get a chance. A voice suddenly called out from the street.

"Say, folks, what kind of animal is that I see over there?"

Brady grinned at Range. Old Mr. McKain must have smelled the news because there he was leaning out of his buggy with his rifle still across his knees.

"Which animal you referring to?" one man called and the rest laughed.

"The four-legged one."

"He's a hound-dog," the man answered.

"Southern hound," someone else added.

Mr. McKain shook his head. "Don't look to me like the northern climate would agree with him." He raised his gun ever so slightly. "I make the motion that hounddog goes back South before something happens to him."

"I second the motion," someone called.

By this time, however, the slave catcher and his dog were already moving down the street. Mr. McKain leaned toward the group of people watching. "Just to be neighborly," he said, "I'm goin' along and see him over the hill." He motioned to Brady and Range. "If you boys are ready to go home, I'll give you a lift as far as my place."

The boys climbed into the buggy and Mr. McKain rose halfway to his feet and flapped the reins at his horse.

"Come on, Daisy," he cried, "we'll drive the enemy over the hills like we always done."

As the buggy caught up to the slave catcher, Mr. McKain slowed his horse to a walk and handed the reins to Brady. He raised his rifle and, pointing it at the slave catcher's back, he began to call out at the top of his voice every verse in the Bible that had fire and brimstone in it. Any man, he ended up, who would keep, buy, sell, or hunt a slave was no better than a murderer. "And we know what to do with them," he

71

shouted. "Redcoats, murderers, traitors, slaveholders, copperheads — we treat 'em all alike."

As Brady bumped over the rough road in the buggy, the picture of his mother's home in Virginia seemed to jog along with him, mixing up his thoughts. His mother's folks weren't the kind of people Mr. McKain was talking about and he felt like telling him so. Instead Brady leaned over to Range.

"You think that slave catcher's through looking for runaways around here, don't you?" he whispered.

Range shrugged. "Who knows?" he said. "That's his job."

The slave catcher was hurrying along beside the buggy, doing his best to ignore Mr. McKain and at the same time trying to prod his dog to a faster pace. The dog, obviously old and overworked, was lagging farther and farther behind until all at once the slave catcher brought out from under his coat a whip. He snapped it in the air and the dog lurched forward with what seemed to be a supreme burst of effort. He began sniffing the ground first to one side and then to the other while the slave catcher kept the whip twitching at his heels.

Brady shivered. The slave catcher looked as if he meant business, all right.

Chapter Six

As Mr. McKain approached his house he grabbed the reins from Brady, but he was shouting so hard at the slave catcher that instead of going into the driveway as he intended, he turned Daisy into the front yard. It surprised her so that she set out for the barn at a gallop, reeling the buggy around the cannon as she

73

went. The boys were thrown against the side of the buggy; Mr. McKain was jerked to his feet.

"Whoa, there, whoa, you crazy old fool," he shouted at Daisy, pulling on the reins until the buggy halted. "Consarn your hide! You almost knocked into my cannon."

The boys glanced back. Polished as always and glistening in the sunlight, the cannon was the only thing around the McKain place that didn't look weatherbeaten. It was a shame it didn't get more use.

"You know, Mr. McKain," Range suggested hopefully, "if you shot off your cannon, you'd scare that slave catcher over the state line in a hurry."

"You sure would," Brady agreed quickly.

But Mr. McKain shook his head. "Naw," he grumbled and eased himself down from the buggy. "I wouldn't waste my cannon on a yellow-bellied varmint like that."

He began unhitching Daisy, and Brady and Range started home. They could see the slave catcher ahead of them, his head bent, walking more slowly now that he'd left Mr. McKain behind and thought he was unobserved. Except for an occasional halfhearted crack of his whip, he gave no indication at the moment that he was hunting slaves or anything else. He went by Post's mill, which was obviously deserted and broken down, a likely hiding place if there ever was one, and gave it no more than a passing glance. Perhaps he had given up, Brady thought, but at that moment a figure broke out of the bushes at the side of the road and changed everything.

It was Laban Williams, running and panting after the slave catcher. He had run all the way from town, staying out of sight, too scared to show his face until Mr. McKain had gone.

"Hey, mister," Laban called. "Maybe I can help."

Range narrowed his eyes and watched Laban catch up to the slave catcher and dance along at his side.

"That Laban can stick his nose into other people's business faster than anybody I know," Range muttered, and he spit into the road. Brady followed suit. It seemed more than they could bear to watch Laban strutting along like a rooster so stuck on himself when what he needed was a good poke in the nose.

"He's liable to go into the woods," Brady said.

"Well, the woods are a big place. If he doesn't already know, he may not even think of Drover's place." Range shifted the package he was carrying from one hand to the other. "Let's just follow the little polecat."

The two boys took to the side of the road, staying out of sight, skirting around the back of farmhouses, peeping from behind barns. If they didn't have the slave catcher and Laban in sight all the while, they were at least able to keep track of them. At one point where the road took a wide curve, Brady and Range cut ahead. It was at a spot where a path turned off the road to go into the woods. They hid behind a thick growth of berry bushes and waited.

Brady lay on his stomach, wishing he had a drink of water and hoping that the slave catcher wouldn't go into the woods. But when the footsteps came, they turned down the path — Laban and the slave catcher. The dog was not with them. He must have been so worn out, Brady thought, that he'd been tied up somewhere to wait for the slave catcher. Laban was in the lead, heading straight for the woods. He had that big black jackknife he was so proud of in his hand and he was throwing it, blade down ahead of him and watching it quiver in the ground. It was rather an unusual knife, Brady had to admit, with curlicues carved on it and a big W for Williams. Still it was nowhere near as wonderful as Laban made out.

"This is a dandy jackknife, all right," Laban was saying as he stooped to pick it up. "Belonged to my great-uncle. He was an Indian fighter. You know what he did? He used this knife once to scalp an Indian."

Laban had all kinds of wild tales he told about that jackknife. Brady and Range had heard them all. They listened to this one until they could no longer hear Laban's voice, then they crawled out and took up the trail again.

Once they were in the woods, their course was easier. They knew this territory in and out. They could slip from cover to cover in the same way they had years ago when they had played scouts and Indians. One of their favorite games had been seeing how close they could come to each other without being detected. Now hiding behind the same rocks, the same trees, they were able from time to time to come within hearing distance of Laban and the slave catcher.

Laban certainly didn't seem to have Drover Hull's place in mind as a destination. He wandered as aimlessly as if he were looking for wild flowers, more interested in telling his tales than anything else. Here and there Brady caught a few phrases and he smiled in relief. Laban Williams didn't know beans and that was a fact. Now he was claiming that his pa was going to be sheriff soon and to get in practice, he often came to these woods to bag himself a runaway or two.

"See this campfire?" Laban pointed to a pile of old ashes. "Runaways have been through here. That's some of their doin's."

Brady and Range, dropped down behind some dead-wood at the foot of a small incline, winked at each other, recalling the time the two of them had built that very fire.

The slave catcher kicked his boot into the ashes. He walked around the old fire, butting his toe into it again and again, stamping on it as if he could see some sparks. Laban didn't appear to be paying any attention. He was leaning up against a tree, his chest puffed out, his eyes dreamy, his jaws working. Suddenly the slave catcher's hand darted out and grabbed Laban by the collar and spun him around. He held him so that his feet were barely touching the ground and his face was within inches of his own.

"I'm sick of your stories," he hissed. Still holding him by the back of the collar as if he were a cat, the slave catcher shook Laban. "For all I know," he said, "you may be a rotten little abolitionist yourself with the notion that it's cute to lead me on a wild-goose chase."

Brady lay flat on his stomach, his mouth drier than dust, and watched an ant crawl across a piece of wood. The surface of the wood was rough and the ant kept slipping into crevices.

"Maybe I don't like to tangle with an abolitionist on a public road," the slave catcher went on, dropping his words one at a time as if he were laying down his whip slow and easy. "But off here in the woods I wouldn't care *what* I did to one." He released Laban so suddenly, he fell backwards to the ground.

"You said you'd lead me to some runaways," the slave catcher snarled. "Now are you or aren't you?"

Brady couldn't bring himself to look at Laban. He watched the ant slowly trying to regain the position it had lost a moment before. It waved its threadlike legs in the air in search of a footing, while a few feet away Laban Williams struggled up, whimpering.

"I know a good place to look," Laban sniveled. "Don't you worry. I'm no abolitionist. I know a place farther on. A little cabin hidden in the trees. A crazy old hermit lives there."

An acorn fell from an oak tree and landed with a thud at Brady's elbow. He looked at Range lying a yard or so away, chewing on a piece of grass. He couldn't tell by Range's expression what he was thinking or whether his heart was beating fast the way Brady's was or his breath coming short. It was one thing to follow

a slave catcher when you weren't sure of the outcome;
it was another thing when you *knew* you were going
to end up at an Underground Railroad station. The
sound of the slave catcher's voice still hung in the air.
"*Off here in the woods,*" he had said, "*I wouldn't care
what I did to one.*"

Brady knew what Matt would say if he were here
now. He'd point out that there was no way in the world
Brady could help the slaves get away. He'd remind him
that he'd got into enough trouble with his pa and then
he'd tell Brady to turn around and go home and mind
his own business.

Range kicked him on the leg. "Come on," he whispered impatiently.

The slave catcher and Laban had gone. Brady listened
for their footsteps but they were so far away, he
couldn't hear them. For a moment Brady thought about
suggesting that they go home, but what would Range
say to that? Probably the same thing he'd say if Brady
ever told him that he didn't care about hunting. Brady
got to his feet, walking softly, just the way Range did.

Now that they knew where they were going, they followed at a safer distance than they had before, planning
to go around to the far side of Drover Hull's clearing
to do their spying where there would be less chance of
being caught. Once they had their plans made, Brady
and Range didn't do much talking. Brady, who usually
stopped to notice every spider web and deer track,
couldn't think of anything now but the clearing that
lay ahead. He pictured the runaways working in the

vegetable garden the way they had been that other day, their brown backs bent over, bare and shining in the sunlight. He pictured the slave catcher stepping suddenly into that clearing, cracking his whip and pulling his pistol out of his belt.

But when they came to the far side of the clearing and looked at last at Drover Hull's cabin, Brady realized that of all possibilities, he had least expected this. There was no sign of life except Laban and the slave catcher standing uncertainly, looking about. Drover's house was closed tight and the windows were boarded up. The rocking chair had been put away, the flag taken down, and even the vegetable garden had been pulled up and dirt scuffled over it. Dead branches had been scattered over the yard and stones and boulders rolled onto it to give the place a deserted, neglected appearance. It was hard to believe that a little while ago smoke had been curling up from the cabin and rows of corn and beans had been growing behind it. If his father could see the place now, Brady thought, he really would think that Brady had been making up tales.

The slave catcher was going around the house, prying at window boards and trying the doors. He had his shoulder against the back door and was pushing at it when Range whispered to Brady to look at what Laban was doing.

At first Brady couldn't see that Laban was doing much of anything except wandering around, kicking at stones and muttering about footprints, but then it became apparent that all the time he was edging closer and closer toward the broomstraw bordering the woods. He kept glancing sideways over his shoulder and all at once, while the slave catcher's back was turned, Laban ducked into the broomstraw and ran. Brady had never known Laban to be so quick and quiet; the slave catcher hadn't even noticed that he had gone.

"Come here and help me," the slave catcher called, trying to force the back door open. "Never mind the footprints, you fool," he shouted when Laban didn't come. "Come here, blast you."

At last the slave catcher turned around and saw that Laban was not in sight. The slave catcher walked quickly to the front of the house, to the edge of the clearing and then disappeared into the woods the way he had come, his language and his whip crackling at the same time. He would never find Laban now, Brady thought, listening to the string of words bubbling and boiling in the slave catcher's wake.

Range and Brady crept down to the cabin. Brady peeked through an opening between two window boards. In the gloomy half-light the room looked as if it had been deserted a long time — indeed, as if it could scarcely remember Drover Hull. The rocking chair was turned upside down in the middle of the room and a spider was already spinning a web between its two rockers.

There was no clue anywhere around the clearing as to what might have happened. Range started home, but before following him, Brady stopped at the well and pulled himself the drink he had been wanting so long.

He dipped the tin cup that had been left by the well into the clear water and drank from it. It was wonderfully cold and refreshing, but at the same time Brady noticed how strange he felt. Maybe he had been feeling that way earlier but he didn't remember. All he knew was that now, as he put the cup down, he felt dizzy and sick, and he had just had a drink from Drover Hull's well. Out of Drover Hull's tin cup, as a matter of fact. The same cup that he had seen Tar Adams drink from a week before.

Chapter Seven

THERE WAS NO DOUBT about it; Brady had a fever.
All the way back home, he knew it but couldn't
bring himself to admit to Range that he'd been foolish
enough to drink out of Drover Hull's tin cup.

Range kept speculating as to what might have happened to Drover and the Underground station. "They
couldn't have been discovered," Range said. "Other-

wise we would have heard about it. You can't keep a piece of news like that quiet."

Brady stumbled along not answering, thinking only how nice it would be to get home and crawl into his bed. But, of course, he wouldn't be able to go to bed — not without answering a lot of questions that he didn't much care to answer. "Where were you when you began to feel sick?" his mother would say. "What were you doing? Did you have anything to eat or drink?" And supposing he came right out and told them the whole story? Well, he'd rather die of a fever than tell his father he'd been following a slave catcher all afternoon and had just come back from spying at Drover Hull's place.

At the supper table Brady thought he really might die; he wondered if Drover's spells were ever strong enough to kill you. He could hardly bring himself to swallow the vegetable soup his mother put in front of him and when he went to spread a slice of bread, his hand trembled so it was a wonder nobody noticed. If it had been Mary Dorcas who was sick, they would have noticed quick enough, Brady thought as he looked across the table at his cousin. She wasn't eating too well either but it was only because she was listening so hard. Brady's father and Uncle Earl were talking about the plans for celebrating Independence Day. It was only a little over two weeks away now, the most important day of the year except maybe Christmas, but Brady felt too poorly to get excited.

"We'll have to plan it carefully," Mr. Minton was

saying, "so one way or another the celebration isn't turned into a riot over slavery."

"That's all Bill Williams is looking for," Uncle Earl grumbled. "He's just aching for an opportunity to say the abolitionists are disturbing the peace and that I'm failing in my duty as sheriff."

Brady remembered what Range had said about Laban Williams' pa, but at the moment his head was hurting so much he couldn't bring himself to repeat it.

"We may be all right if we can just keep old Mr. McKain quiet," Mr. Minton said. "I tell you what. We'll ask him to open the program by reading the Declaration of Independence. That way he'll have his chance to talk and we can be sure just what he's going to say."

Brady's father and his Uncle Earl laughed and began to tackle their food again, but Mary Dorcas pushed her plate aside. This wasn't the part of Independence Day that interested her.

"Will there be floats?" she asked.

Mr. and Mrs. Minton looked at each other across the table and smiled. "We're planning on two or three," Mr. Minton said.

"Will there be ladies all dressed up riding on the floats?"

"Ladies and girls," Mr. Minton said, looking again at his wife rather than at Mary Dorcas. Mrs. Minton nodded her head as if to agree to something that hadn't been said.

"The Pennsylvania float will be decorated with

roses," Mr. Minton went on, "and sitting under a flowered parasol will be a young lady. I believe, if I remember rightly, the committee is to ask a certain young
lady by the name of Mary Dorcas Minton."

Brady didn't see Mary Dorcas' face light up. All of
a sudden it seemed to him that he saw her flowered
parasol turning and turning on the float. Faster and
faster. Then there were other parasols and they were
all turning and Brady was turning with them.

"Why, Brady Minton," he heard his mother say, "I
believe you're sick."

He felt her hand on his head and then he felt his
father lifting him and carrying him up the stairs to his
bed. As his mother took off his shoes, he could hear her
voice coming from what seemed a long way off. "Just
what I expected," she said. "It would have been a miracle
if it hadn't happened. He's coming down with measles
that he caught from Mary Dorcas."

For several days Brady's fever was so high that his
dreams kept getting mixed up with what was really
going on around him. Once through the open register
in his floor he heard his father's and his uncle's voices in
the dining room below. They were saying that Mr.
Williams had announced that he was running for sheriff
against Earl Minton. They were anticipating that Mr.
Williams would be trying to show himself off on Independence Day and do everything in his power to put
Uncle Earl in a bad light. All at once in the middle of
listening to this conversation, it seemed to Brady that
Mr. Williams turned into the slave catcher and was

chasing him with his whip, and Laban, his eyes red and watery like the bloodhound's, was dancing along behind. Brady could feel the whip cutting his legs as he tried to run faster. Then the first thing he knew he was in some kind of underground tunnel and at the end of the tunnel was the scarecrow he'd put up in the cornfield. Only it wasn't the scarecrow; it was Drover Hull, his white hair standing on end and his eyes wild. "Tattletale," Drover said as he came near. "Tattletale." He said it over and over and his voice sounded hollow in the tunnel.

When Brady woke up, his mother was sitting beside him bathing his forehead, and Mary Dorcas was standing in the doorway in a long, half-finished pink and white ruffled affair that she was apparently planning to wear on Independence Day.

"Now he'll be better," Mrs. Minton was saying. "His fever's broken. Just look at all those spots that have come out."

"He has lots more than I had," Mary Dorcas said and her eyes were big and scared-looking. "He's lots sicker than I was, isn't he, Auntie?"

Good, Brady thought. Good. Although he could feel the cool breeze coming in the window and knew for the first time that he was, indeed, better, he half closed his eyes and in a weak voice asked Mary Dorcas if she would mind bringing him a glass of cool buttermilk.

Brady's mother moved his bed over by the window and, although Brady would never have admitted it, he found it was rather enjoyable to lie there, listening to someone else cut wood, eating all kinds of good things made especially to please him, and thinking up new errands for Mary Dorcas to do. For a while it worried him that perhaps when he'd been so sick, he had talked out about Drover Hull, but he guessed he hadn't because his father was very kind, even promising that he and Range could each drive a float in the Independence Day parade. All he had to do now, his father said, was to lie still and get well, but as the days went on, that became pretty tiring. As a matter of fact, there came a day when he had had just about enough. Try as he might, he couldn't even think of another thing to ask Mary Dorcas to do. She was always so eager to wait on him, so pleased to do whatever he wanted. And his mother would pat Mary Dorcas on the head and say, "Isn't she the *best* little nurse?" It made Brady want to think of a job that was really challenging. If, for instance, he could ask Mary Dorcas to go out and dig up a handful of fishing worms, he knew he would feel better, but of course there was no sense to that and his mother would put a stop to it anyway.

Brady looked out the window. Way down the hill, he could just make out the shape of his scarecrow in the cornfield, one skinny arm pointing to the north and the other to the south as if it were asking you to make up your mind. As he looked at it, the thought of Mary Dorcas came creeping back to him, and the thought of Drover Hull too. It put him in mind of several interesting possibilities to keep Mary Dorcas busy, but the trouble was his mother would stop them all. It was a pity. Still, there was a long afternoon ahead and he could at least give Mary Dorcas something to think about.

"Mary Dorcas!" he called. "Mary Dorcas!"

As Mary Dorcas came hurrying into the room, Brady leaned out from his bed and put his finger to his lips. "Listen," he whispered tensely.

Obediently Mary Dorcas stopped where she was and stood still, but it was clear that she couldn't hear anything exceptional. The grasshoppers were sawing away as usual outside; Mrs. Minton was rattling dishes in the kitchen; Brady's father and uncle were going over figures at the dining room table. He could hear the murmur of their voices coming up through the register from time to time. There was nothing out of the way. Still, whenever Mary Dorcas started to speak or move forward, Brady stopped her. "Sh, sh," he whispered, holding up his hand and cocking his head toward the window. After a few minutes Brady shrugged his shoulders.

"Shucks," he said. "I guess it's stopped. I thought if you got here fast enough, you could hear it too."

Mary Dorcas moved over and looked out the window. "What was it?" she asked.

"Oh, it was the scarecrow again." Brady sighed as if he had put up with that scarecrow as long as he could. "Every time the wind blows just right, you can hear it. Moaning and groaning and carrying on something fierce."

Mary Dorcas shook back her curls. "Oh, Brady Minton," she said, "there you go, teasing me again."

If it had been any other girl shaking back her curls like that, Brady might have given up, but not with Mary Dorcas. He had seen her before, acting smart one minute and the next willing to believe you if you told her a polecat was a house kitty. Brady set his face to appear as straight and true as if he were in church. He looked Mary Dorcas square in the eye.

"Now why would I tease about a thing as serious as that?" he asked. "That scarecrow is plainly bewitched. All I wanted to do was to get you to hear it for yourself so you'd know not to go near it." He shook his head. "I should have known you wouldn't believe me. There's bewitchment loose all over the place, but likely you're the type of person that will have to be hit yourself before you'll take anyone's word for it."

Mary Dorcas was standing at the head of Brady's bed, looking out the window. She didn't turn around.

"What do you mean — there's bewitchment loose?" she asked.

Brady grinned to himself. "Well, now, maybe you've noticed some of it," he said. "A lot of little things mysteriously going wrong. I heard Ma say the butter wouldn't come when she churned yesterday. Isn't that so?"

Mary Dorcas nodded.

"Both the horses took a notion yesterday they didn't want to be harnessed. Right from this window I watched

Pa struggle with them. And Uncle Earl knocked over a pot of coffee on the stove. Of course," Brady said, "I'm up here in bed and don't know all that's going on. You probably know more than I do if you put your mind to it."

Mary Dorcas turned around and her eyes were as big as doorknobs.

"Auntie's bread took the longest time to rise yesterday," she whispered. "And I skinned my knee."

Brady spread his hands apart. "See?" he said. "What did I tell you? Bewitchment all over the place. Some of Drover Hull's doing, most likely. Now that he's shut up his cabin, he must be hiding nearby, practicing his different spells."

As he watched Mary Dorcas' face, Brady persuaded himself that deep down he'd never really been taken in by any of that nonsense about Drover Hull and his spells. As for ever being scared himself, he put it right out of his mind.

"How do you know Drover shut up his cabin?" Mary Dorcas asked.

"We saw it." Brady raised his voice in confidence as he became convinced that in spite of her questions, Mary Dorcas had already swallowed the bait. Hook, line, and sinker, he chuckled to himself. "Range and I were over there the day I got sick. As a matter of fact, we were following a slave catcher. Of course we knew good and well there were runaways hiding over at Drover's place, so we hung around to see what would happen. But they had gone and Drover's cabin was boarded up, the way I told you."

Mary Dorcas sat down on the edge of Brady's bed. She looked into her lap and rolled the edge of her apron up and then flattened it down again. It surely was interesting, Brady thought, to observe how easy it was to frighten a girl.

"Do you know for sure that Drover Hull can cast spells?" Mary Dorcas asked.

Hook, line, and sinker, Brady repeated to himself, sitting up in bed and hugging his knees. "Of course. I've seen him do it. Why, one time that Range and I were over there, we watched him cast a spell on Tar Adams. It just so happened that this particular spell was a good spell, but good or bad, he can do them all."

Brady let his mind go back to the day he and Range had crouched behind the broomstraw. Of course, they hadn't seen Drover actually casting a spell, but as Brady sneaked a look at Mary Dorcas' expectant face, he thought it would be a shame to stick too close to facts. "It makes my flesh crawl to think of it," he said reflectively. "Especially now when I'm sick, but I'll try and tell you anyway." He hesitated a moment. "Well, there was Tar Adams hobbling around the cabin on his crutches. No one else was around. Then all of a sudden Drover came out of the house, into the back yard, and he took his shoes off. He dipped a tin cup into the well beside the house and began sprinkling water around in a circle." As Brady watched Mary Dorcas' eyes grow rounder, he warmed up to his story. "When all the water was gone, he began dancing around that circle, saying a lot of queer-sounding words, and every once in a while he'd spit. You know what happened then? Tar Adams threw his crutches down on the ground and walked on his legs as natural as could be. The fact is, he kind of sprinted around the clearing just to see how it felt."

Mary Dorcas' eyes never left Brady's face during the time he was telling the story and even when he had finished, she didn't move. It looked to Brady as if she were still in that clearing, watching Drover Hull dance. When at last she did speak, her voice was shaky.

"You don't suppose, do you," she asked, "that the scarecrow will start moaning and groaning in the night so that I'll hear it?"

Brady looked thoughtfully out the window for a moment and then he shrugged. "Who knows?" he said. "I just hope that once it gets dark, it doesn't start *walking*."

After Mary Dorcas had gone out of the room, Brady leaned back on his pillows and grinned. She was scared silly and that was a fact. He pictured her afraid to turn every corner for fear she'd find Drover Hull lurking on the other side. Tonight she'd likely lie in the dark hour after hour, listening for that fool scarecrow. Brady had a couple more days he had to stay in bed, but now the prospect didn't seem so had. With the material he had started on, he figured he could keep himself entertained in good style. He was planning his next conversation with Mary Dorcas when he heard his father and his uncle scrape their chairs back from the dining room table.

"Mary Dorcas," he heard his uncle say, "come here a minute. I want to straighten you out on something." His voice came through the register clear as a bell.

All at once Brady felt his face grow hot. His body stiffened and he broke into a sweat as he heard his father's footsteps on the stairs and realized that sound could travel just as easily down the register as it could travel up. Not only had he made up a lot of wild tales; he'd talked about the Underground Railroad again, about the runaways and Drover Hull and Tar Adams. He had even admitted he'd been over there the day he took sick. Brady closed his eyes and prayed that he could go back and find himself in one of his measles nightmares again.

When he opened his eyes, his father was standing in the doorway. Indeed, he seemed to be filling the entire doorway and his face looked dark, the way it did when he was preaching about sin. Brady braced himself for the thunder of his father's words but when he spoke, his voice was low and tight-sounding and somehow harder to bear.

"If you were not sick," his father said slowly, "you would receive a thrashing you would not easily forget. As it is, we better not trust you off the farm this summer unless we can keep an eye on you all the time."

He turned and left the room and it seemed to Brady that the whole beautiful summer slipped out the door with his father. Now he would never be able to go to Washington to see Matt. He might even have to stay home on Independence Day. Worse than that, Brady thought as he turned his face to the wall, his father would never trust him again. And all because he didn't have the good sense to keep his mouth shut.

Chapter Eight

NO ONE SPOKE to Brady about his punishment, but they didn't need to. Brady could read the knowledge in his mother's eyes whenever she looked at him. Even after he was up and helping with the chores, his mother's eyes worried at him, wondering, it seemed to Brady, how a boy with all those faults would ever amount to a hill of beans. And Mary Dorcas treated him as if he were still sick. Instead of holding those wild tales against him, she acted sorry, for petey's sakes, offering to help him with his work. A person with any natural feeling, Brady thought, would take some pleasure in watching a fellow get punished for scaring the living daylights out of him, but not Mary Dorcas. Her moony eyes and her sweet ways were like nettles under Brady's skin. "Leave me be," he would snap at her. Later if he began to feel guilty for his orneriness, all he needed to do was remind himself that any time she wanted, Mary Dorcas could run and listen to his mother talk about how she'd always wanted a girl.

But it was his father's attitude that Brady minded most. It seemed to Brady that his father never quite looked at him. Brady would ask his father if he'd like some help with the stumps in the lower pasture or with the repair work on the barn roof, but his father's glance would slide right off him and he would say no, Brady had better content himself with gathering the eggs. Of course his father might be just sparing him because of having been sick, but on the other hand, Brady sometimes wondered if his father would ever trust him with a man's work again.

Brady couldn't talk to his father at all. For one thing, Mr. Minton's mind was too much occupied with the Independence Day proceedings. The rumor was now that Mr. Williams and his group were determined to turn the program into a free-for-all and then blame Earl Minton for not keeping the peace. As it happened, the Independence Day committee was composed entirely of anti-slavery men headed up by Brady's father and uncle, so all Mr. Williams really had to do was to pounce on the first word that might sound like anti-slavery talk, then claim the committee was using a patriotic occasion to promote its treasonous ideas. He'd say, too, that Earl Minton was behind it and wasn't fit to be sheriff. He'd stand up tall and slinky, the way he was, with a smile on his weasel-like face, and tell people if they wanted law and order, they ought to vote for him, Bill Williams. Already he had nailed to fences up and down the road posters, asking for votes.

One morning Brady had found a poster on their own barn, nailed up during the night. As Brady went out to the cows, Mr. Williams' name jumped out at him from a piece of white paper on the barn door. ELECT A MAN FOR SHERIFF, the paper said. VOTE FOR BILL WILLIAMS. *Man* was written bigger and blacker than the other words. Brady tore the paper down and ground his heel in Mr. Williams' name. "They have to say *man*," Brady muttered. "Otherwise you wouldn't know." He smashed his foot down on the paper again and again.

It was no wonder that as Independence Day drew closer, everyone in the Minton household became more tense. Not only were the men concerned over what Mr. Williams might do, Mrs. Minton and Mary Dorcas were in a fluster over costumes, decorations, and food for the community picnic following the program. Matt was coming home for the celebration. Brady's grandmother, his Uncle Will and Aunt Sadie were all driving down and planning to take Mary Dorcas back with them for a visit. There was so much preparation going on, a person had to be careful or he'd trip over a festoon of ribbon stretched across the floor or knock into a pie set out for cooling.

And Brady still didn't know if he'd be allowed to attend the celebration at all. The first time his pa made a joke, Brady decided, he'd ask him outright. If, for instance, after a meal, his father would tip back his chair and stretch his legs out long, the way he did sometimes when he felt easy, and say, "Well, that was a good sample. Where's the meal?", then Brady would know it was the right time to ask. But it didn't appear that his father would ever feel that easy. The night of July third, Brady went to bed, not knowing.

When he came down to breakfast the next morning, he had all but given up hope. Everyone was intent on his own business. It was not until after morning prayers that Mr. Minton even glanced in Brady's direction. Then as they were leaving the table, Mr. Minton leaned down and picked up from the floor a tall silk hat he'd apparently been concealing. He spun the hat across the room to Brady.

"That's what you're to wear today, boy, when you drive the Virginia float," he said. For the first time in days there seemed to be a twinkle in his eyes. "I figure that as long as Matt is home, he can keep his eyes on you. Or what is more to the point, his ears. Just don't go off on your own."

Even the fact that his father referred to Brady's disgrace in front of Matt and his grandmother and all the rest of them, even that fact could not at the moment dampen Brady's suddenly soaring spirits. He cocked the tall hat on his head at a jaunty angle and walked out of the room, whistling "Yankee Doodle." He burst into song, making up his own words as he went along.

"Brady Minton went to town," he sang, tipping his hat to his grandmother as he went through the kitchen.

> "Paradin' fit to kill,
> Drove a dec-o-ra-ted float
> Up and down a hill."

The parade formed outside of town at Mr. McKain's house, as it did every year. Horses and floats and flags and fifers and drummers and riflemen and veterans and children and parasols were all over the place. Presiding over the confusion, riding on a white horse, was Mr. McKain in a three-cornered hat, self-appointed director of activity. He was slashing a sword in the air as Brady and Range and Matt approached.

"To your stations, men," he shouted. "Mount your steeds!" When no one paid any attention, he raised his voice. "To your stations — " he began but broke off in the middle of his order. He pointed his sword at Brady. "Get those blame children off my cannon," he roared.

Three small boys were straddling Mr. McKain's cannon, bouncing up and down and shouting "Giddyup!" As Brady went to remove them, he could hear Mr. McKain carrying on about how did they expect to get anywhere with all these durn fool women and children hanging around. "Can't even see where the rifle company is with all them fancy petticoats stuck in the air," he grumbled, referring to the ladies' parasols. Old Mr. McKain was riding high, Brady thought, yanking a youngster by the seat of his pants off the cannon. It was going to be hard to hold a man like that down once the program got started.

In spite of Mr. McKain, the parade finally formed. Brady found himself holding the reins to a pair of shiny black horses and behind him was the prettiest float in the parade. The entire float was covered with real grass to look like a lawn, and in the center there was a model of George Washington's home in Virginia with exactly the right number of white pillars. Standing beside the model, towering over it, as a matter of fact, was Mr. Minton's best friend, Mr. Emmett Fergus, taking the part of George Washington and, strangely enough, even bearing him some resemblance. There were a couple of parasol girls on the front lawn, giggling and throwing kisses right and left.

In front of Brady, Range drove the Pennsylvania float with another of Mr. Minton's friends, Dr. Scott, taking the part of William Penn. Farther in front were the veterans of the War of Independence led by Mr. McKain on his white charger. There weren't many veterans left now and all of them were pretty feeble except for Mr. McKain, who would never run out of energy, Brady guessed, not if he lived to be a hundred. The rifle company was up there too and leading the parade was the Fife and Drum Corps, sending back the sweetest marching music you'd ever hope to hear. It was all Brady could do to keep himself sitting still in his driver's seat. "Brady Minton went to town," he hummed, "paradin' fit to kill." It didn't make Brady feel any worse either when a few minutes later in front of the Jackson Hotel he caught sight of Laban Williams, standing with a line of onlookers, gaping at him in his high silk hat.

Laban stepped out from the crowd and walked beside the Virginia float for a few paces.

"Well, what do you know!" Laban leered. "Brady Minton driving a float from one of those evil, slave-holding states!"

"And what do *you* know!" Brady returned. "Laban Williams standing on the sidelines, gawking!" Brady tipped his hat and drove on, grinning.

After they reached the picnic ground, however, where the town had assembled for the program, Brady began to feel uneasy. At first glance everything looked just the way it should. The floats were drawn up behind the platform, which was decorated with red, white, and blue streamers. The rifle company stood to one side, ready to fire their thirteen salutes, one for each of the original states of the Union. The veterans were seated in places of honor on the platform. For the moment Mr. McKain looked surprisingly cool and controlled. Even the weather was behaving itself — a bright blue sky with only a puff or two of white clouds such as a cannon might have fired in celebration. Still, as

Brady walked among the crowd, he had the distinct impression that folks were on edge, waiting for something more than the usual Fourth of July doings. Some of Bill Williams' posters were nailed on the trees, and then Brady noticed Bill Williams himself. Instead of standing with his friends, laughing and talking as you might expect, Bill Williams was standing alone at the side of the crowd, his arms folded over his chest. His friends — Brady picked them out one by one — were scattered through the audience, each standing alone. And Bill Williams was wearing around his waist a belt with a gun in it, as if he were already sheriff. Aside from the rifle company and Uncle Earl, he was the only man in the crowd to carry a gun.

Brady joined Matt and Range at the back of the field. Matt was frowning. "I don't like the looks of things," he said. "Anyone looking for trouble as hard as Bill Williams is bound to find it."

Mr. Minton opened the program with a prayer. At his side Old Glory waved its stars and stripes gently in the breeze.

"Bless this great land of ours," Mr. Minton said.

Brady opened his eyes and looked over the bowing heads. Laban Williams had his eyes open too. He was sneaking up to his father.

"Bless our President," Mr. Minton said.

Laban and his father whispered throughout the prayer. They didn't take notice again until Mr. Minton was introducing Mr. McKain and saying what a pleasure it was to have on the program an old soldier who had played a part in the fight for independence. Mr. Minton described all the campaigns Mr. McKain had participated in. He talked for so long about everything Mr. McKain had done in the past that he neglected to mention that what Mr. McKain was going to do now was to read the Declaration of Independence. But of course, as soon as Mr. McKain began, everyone would know what he was reading.

Brady looked over at Mr. Williams. His head was jutting forward and his narrow eyes were like a cat's as Mr. McKain stepped up and began, "When in the course of human events . . ."

Brady expected Mr. Williams to settle back as soon as he heard the familiar words, but he didn't. He said something out of the corner of his mouth to Laban and moved closer so as not to miss a word. He jutted his neck out and shifted his weight from one foot to another, the way a cat does, waiting for the right moment to pounce. Brady glanced at Matt and saw that he was grinning.

"He doesn't recognize it," Matt whispered, his eyes twinkling. "He doesn't know it's the Declaration of Independence. He thinks it's some kind of abolitionist talk."

Matt edged over behind Bill Williams. Brady and Range followed.

"We'll have some fun," Matt whispered again. "Maybe we can get him to show himself up for the ignorant fool he is."

". . . a decent respect for the opinions of mankind . . ."

Mr. McKain was repeating the words at the top of his lungs with all the dramatic fervor that he so enjoyed.

Matt nudged Brady and drew a long face. "Shucks," he whispered in a tone that Bill Williams could not help but overhear. "I told Pa Mr. McKain would talk out of turn and cause trouble."

Bill Williams pulled in his neck and poked Laban.

Brady winked at his brother. "Oh-oh," he whispered, "Mr. McKain's going too far. Why doesn't he stick to the War of Independence?"

"Folks aren't goin' to like that kind of talk," Range agreed.

Mr. McKain was flinging himself into the spirit of the occasion. "We hold these truths to be self-evident," he shouted, shaking his fist as if George the Third were out in front and going to give him an argument. "All men are created equal . . ."

Bill Williams shuffled around restlessly.

". . . they are endowed by their Creator with certain unalienable Rights . . ."

Suddenly Bill Williams, with a nod toward his friends, raised his voice. "We don't want to hear any of that stuff," he shouted belligerently, hiking up his belt and starting to move toward the platform.

"Treason, treason, slander, troublemaker!" Laban screamed, jumping up and down in excitement.

For a moment the crowd was too surprised to say or do anything. Then all at once everyone broke right out loud laughing at a man so ignorant that he not only didn't recognize the Declaration of Independence but was suspicious of it as well. Pro-slavery and anti-slavery people joined together in the fun over it, and Dr. Scott rocked back and forth in his seat on the platform, slapping his knee. Even Mr. Fergus, who was supposed to be in favor of slavery, smiled. By the time the crowd settled down to enjoy the program again, all the uneasiness had slipped away and somehow, Bill and Laban Williams had slipped away too.

"I bet my bottom dollar," Matt said, "this is one day Bill Williams didn't win any new votes."

Brady grinned. He looked up front at his father and uncle. Their relief and amusement showed even in the set of their shoulders as they listened to Mr. McKain conclude his reading.

Dutifully then, Mr. McKain sat down, although everyone could see it wasn't easy for him to give up the center of the stage. The excitement of the day and the joking over Bill Williams had stirred him up so that he fidgeted like a schoolboy through the rest of the program. As soon as it was over, he mounted his white horse.

"The pursuit of happiness!" he shouted, brandishing his sword again. "What I say is — let's pursue it!"

Even during the horseshoe games and the races, Mr. McKain stayed on his horse, exploding with bursts of patriotism, nor could he be coaxed aside by the other veterans, sitting under trees, content to swap yarns more quietly. It was as if he couldn't get all the fire out of his system. As a matter of fact, he was still going strong in the evening on the way home as he rode his horse alongside of Matt, Range, Brady and a wagonload of young people.

> "Turkey in the straw,
> ha, ha, ha,
> Turkey in the hay,
> hey, hey, hey — "

Mr. McKain and the young folks sang together but the closer they came to Mr. McKain's house, the louder and more boisterous Mr. McKain became.

He hates like poison to see the day end, Brady thought, looking at Mr. McKain jogging along, his three-cornered hat pushed back on his head, his elbows clacking up and down in time to the song. Suddenly Brady felt sorry. Mr. McKain was such a spry old man, you didn't stop to think that there were likely not many Independence Days ahead for him.

He was raising his hat now to say good-by as they approached his house, but then all at once, as unexpectedly as if he'd lit upon a gold mine, he threw back his head and let loose a great roll of laughter.

"Now you folks ain't goin' on just yet," he called. "We ain't finished with the day — not by a long shot. Pull up your horses and set a spell."

Whatever Mr. McKain's idea was, he was certainly tickled with it. Still chuckling, he rode his horse into the barn, came out, and went scurrying through his cellar door.

"Now what's he up to?" Matt said. "If it were cider

time of year, I'd think he was going to roll out a barrel."

"It beats me," Range agreed.

A lopsided moon pushed itself over a hill and threw a streamer of light that, as Brady watched, fell across Mr. McKain's yard and smack across his cannon.

Brady looked at Range. "Do you suppose — " he began, but he never finished his sentence. Mr. McKain was back, rolling cannon balls across the yard.

"Come on, fellers," he shouted. "We're a-goin' to wake up George the Third in his grave and set his teeth to rattlin'!"

It was almost too good to believe. Brady had to pinch himself, standing on the stubbly lawn, fireflies flickering all around while Mr. McKain rammed powder down the muzzle of his cannon. Watching him, Brady was suddenly glad Mr. McKain hadn't been in the habit of firing his cannon for any old excuse but instead had waited for a night such as this.

Mr. McKain pointed the cannon at the moon and stepped back to light the torch. Brady felt his skin prickling as he waited for the explosion. Down by the creek the frogs were grumbling deep in their throats; a whippoorwill cried shrilly.

Mr. McKain stood still a moment, his torch aflame, and eyed the moon. "Bet we can knock that old man up there into a cocked hat," he said.

He applied the torch to the powder and the cannon exploded with a thunderous boom that seconds later was still roaring around the hillsides and rumbling along the surface of the ground. It wasn't a noise you heard with just your ears, Brady thought, grinning; you felt it with all your body. Deep inside, you rocked with it. He looked up into the sky and was almost surprised to see the moon still there.

Already Mr. McKain was back, ramming more powder down the cannon. "Again!" he shouted.

Three times he fired the cannon and each time the sound was more glorious than the time before. When the wagonload of young folks at last drove off, Brady looked back at the small, thin figure of Mr. McKain. He was standing among the fireflies beside his cannon, his eyes dreamy, looking at the moon as if he were still listening to the last echoes in the hills.

It seemed to Brady that he could hear those echoes all the way home. The folks were gathered in the kitchen when he and Matt walked in. They were reviewing the day and laughing again over Bill Williams making a monkey of himself.

"I'm so happy everything went off smoothly," Mrs. Minton said as she passed a plate of cookies around. "If there's one thing I purely despise, it's a fuss in public." She passed the plate to her husband. "I thank my lucky stars that you're a man who can have strong opinions on disagreeable subjects without feeling the need of spouting them off in a crowd."

Brady was sitting on a low stool in front of the stove, picking the raisins out of his cookie to eat at the last. He looked up at his father and it seemed to him that a shadow passed over his father's face.

"I preach against sin, don't I?" his father said.

"Oh, but that's different," his mother said. "Everyone's agreed about that."

"Even though they don't always act like it," Brady's grandmother added, taking a cookie. "My, these are tasty," she said.

"Slavery is a sin," Mr. Minton said, his voice icy. Then he began to quote from the Scripture. "For everything there is a season, and a time for every purpose under heaven. There is a time to keep silence and a time to speak."

Now why did Pa's voice have to come out so cold and forbidding, Brady thought, right at cookie time when everyone was happy?

Chapter Nine

THE SUMMER seemed long and empty to Brady when
he woke up the next morning. Independence Day
was over, gone and done with, and nothing lay ahead —
no outing, no walk in the woods, no trip to town, no
excursion to Washington, no holiday of any kind. "We
better not trust you off this farm this summer," his

father had said, "unless we can keep an eye on you."
When you stopped to think about it, the farm was a
mighty small place.

Brady got out of bed and slipped into a shirt and
fresh pair of overalls. He looked over at Matt, lying
back, his head on his arms, staring at the ceiling.

"Do you think Pa would weaken about me coming to
Washington alone?" Brady asked.

Matt didn't move. "You know Pa," he said. "It would
take an emergency of some magnitude to make him
change his mind."

"Supposing I was to be real good?" Brady insisted.
"Supposing I did every last thing just about perfect? If
I worked extra hard and was mannerly and didn't talk
out of turn, then what do you think?"

Matt stretched himself and rolled out of bed. "Well,
you could try," he said. "It wouldn't do any harm to
try."

But when Brady went downstairs, almost the first
thing he was tempted to do was to be unmannerly. Mr.
Parley Potter was sitting on the settee in the dining
room, showing Mary Dorcas his fancy gold watch with
the seventeen jewels.

Brady stopped in the doorway. If there was one
thing he didn't feel like doing, it was mental arithmetic.

"Good morning, Mr. Potter," he said.

"Why, hello, son," Mr. Potter boomed. "I'm just
showing your sister here my watch."

"My cousin," Brady corrected. Then remembering

his resolution, he looked at his father and added quickly, "Sir."

"Well, if I were you, I'd claim she was my sister. Any girl as pretty as this living under the same roof." Mr. Potter chucked Mary Dorcas under the chin and laughed to see her blush. "Pretty as a picture now, isn't she, Brady?"

Brady swallowed hard. "Yes, sir," he said weakly. The words stuck in his throat like two chunks of green apple.

Mr. Potter dropped his watch into the right-hand pocket of his waistcoat and reached into the left-hand pocket and drew out a silver shilling.

"Now this," he said to Mary Dorcas, "is the luckiest thing I own. It's the first piece of money that was ever given me. I never spent it and never will. You hang onto your first piece of money like that and you'll never be poor. It will bring you luck all your life." He spun the coin in the air and caught it. "I suppose you spent your first piece long ago."

Mary Dorcas nodded.

"Too bad," Mr. Potter observed. "Somebody should have told you." He put the shilling back in his pocket, stood up, and slapped Brady on the shoulder.

"Surprised to see me, boy?" he asked. "I had a hankerin' for some of your mother's griddlecakes, so I slipped in during the night. Didn't arouse you, did I? How's the mental arithmetic?" He waved his hand toward the platters of griddlecakes Brady's mother and grandmother were setting on the table. "Take four hundred and fifty-six of those delicious, delectable golden griddlecakes and add to them another nine hundred and thirty-five. What would you have?"

"A bellyache." That's what Brady wanted to say, but instead he closed his eyes and tried to pretend the problem was on his slate at school. He had just about written the numbers down in white chalk when Mary Dorcas answered.

"One thousand, four hundred and ninety-two," she said.

Mr. Parley Potter whooped. "Listen to that!" he cried. "Oh, Brady Minton, you'll never get to be President, letting your little sister get ahead of you like that!"

"Cousin." Brady set his mouth in a straight line and said it under his breath. He didn't believe his manners were going to hold out much longer.

But after a breakfast of griddlecakes, Brady felt better. He wasn't going to let Mr. Potter stand in the way of his plan to impress his father. He took the kitchen bucket out to the pump and filled it with water. Then with a sidelong glance at his father, he announced that he was going out to the woodpile to chop wood. Between blows of his ax, Brady watched his father and his Uncle Will and Mr. Potter walk down to the lower field, talking as earnestly as if they had business to perform. Brady was glad Mr. Potter wasn't staying long. And doubly glad that at any moment Mary Dorcas would be leaving for her visit with Uncle Will.

Brady didn't put his ax down until he saw his father

and mother and Uncle Earl out in front, ready to say good-by to the folks that were going. Mr. Potter was taking the road south. Matt was riding as far as Washington with Uncle Will, and the rest of them going north. Uncle Will and Matt sat in the front seat of the buggy; Brady's grandmother, Aunt Sadie, and Mary Dorcas sat in the back.

"Mind you wear something on your head, Mary Dorcas, whenever you go out," Brady's mother called.

Uncle Will turned to Brady's father. "We'll be ready to see you three weeks from today," he said.

"In three weeks." Mr. Minton nodded solemnly.

Mr. Potter stood beside the buggy with Brady. He jabbed Brady in the ribs. "That sister of yours — she's some looker, eh?"

Brady grunted. Then, as if there hadn't been enough to happen to try Brady's patience, all of a sudden out of a clear sky Mary Dorcas jumped out of the buggy and ran up to him. "I'm going to miss you," she said, and before Brady knew what she was up to, she stood on her tiptoes and kissed him, for petey's sakes. Then she ran back to the buggy and Uncle Will clucked at the horses to move on.

Mr. Potter slapped his bulging waistcoat. "Cousin, eh?" he shouted. "Kissin' cousin, I reckon! You'll do all right, boy! You may get into the White House yet. You may not even need to know arithmetic at all, by George!"

Brady could hear Mr. Potter still laughing as he got into his wagon and headed it south. Brady's face was a flaming red as he returned to the woodpile. He picked up the ax and swung wildly into the wood. *That* for Mary Dorcas, he said. *That* for all girls. And *that* for Mr. Parley Potter. Take that and that and *that*. He let up a minute as he thought back over the incident at the buggy. One thing was sure. He couldn't take credit for holding his tongue that time. If he hadn't been so taken aback, he surely would have lashed out at Mary Dorcas and at Mr. Potter too, and in a most unmannerly way. In fact, he wished he had. He swung down on another log. He most assuredly wished he had.

Several days later, however, Brady admitted that it was a good thing he hadn't talked back. Up to now, as far as he could see, his record was pretty nearly perfect, although it was true that his father hadn't remarked on it. As a matter of fact, his father wasn't around much. For some reason he seemed to be spending an undue amount of time in the Sermon House, but surely, Brady reasoned, in-between times he must have noted that Brady had mended his ways. Surely he had seen those stumps dug up from the pasture. Surely he had noticed how quietly Brady sat at the table. Any time now his father would call him aside and say that in his opinion there was no sense at all in continuing to punish a boy who had already learned his lesson. His father would look him in the eye then, man to man, and tell him he was free.

But the days went by full of good deeds and good manners, each one depressingly like the one before, and still Mr. Minton said nothing. When the next Sunday rolled around, Brady was almost glad to go to church. Things had come to a pretty pass indeed, Brady told himself as he sat down in the pew between his mother and Uncle Earl, when the only way to get off the farm was to go to church.

During the first part of the service Brady occupied himself with looking at the other folks in the congregation. He watched a fly crawl across the back of Dr. Scott's bald head. He leaned forward to see if he could catch the breeze from the fan Mrs. Scott was waving back and forth across her face. It was a hot day. Most of the women were working their fans. The men from time to time were passing their handkerchiefs over their brows — all but Mr. Emmett Fergus. He sat on the other side of the room, serene-looking as always. He was one of those gentlemen you couldn't imagine ever being mussed up or out of sorts or unpleasant. Even in repose his face retained traces of his kindly smile. Everyone liked Mr. Fergus; he was what Mr. Minton called "the salt of the earth."

Sitting behind Mr. Fergus was a different sort of person altogether. It was Laban Williams. He sat with his mother and his two younger brothers. His father rarely attended church. For a while Brady studied Laban, his yellow hair smacked down like a mat of wet fur and his hands folded so saintly in his lap; then because the sight turned his stomach, Brady looked away and began playing the old snow game.

He had invented this game one hot Sunday years ago; he couldn't have been more than six or seven, but even now it was as good a way to pass the time in church as any other. You sat still in your pew and no one suspected that what you were really doing was pretending to make it snow outside. You half closed your eyes and looked through your lashes out the church window and pictured the snow, at first a few flakes fluttering down. The longer you played the game, the colder the world grew, until with practice you were able to imagine the snow drifting up against the church window and then into the church itself — down the aisles, deeper and deeper until at last it lay heavy and quiet, level with the pews. In the end, if the game went well, icicles hung from the church beams and Mr. Minton's breath hovered in a cloud over the congregation. Today as Brady played amid the fanning women and perspiring men, he succeeded in imagining the church to be as cold as the North Pole where, according to one of his father's books, a man's spit froze and turned into a hailstone before it could hit the ground. Brady was picturing just how it would be if your spit froze like that, when his father began his sermon.

"For everything there is a season," his father said . . . "a time to keep silence and a time to speak."

Brady looked at his father through his frozen eyelashes. Where had he heard that verse quoted recently? He began to pile the snow around the pulpit. Then he felt his mother stiffen beside him. Her hands, folded quietly in her lap a moment before, tightened until the knuckles showed white.

Mr. Minton was preaching a sermon against slavery.

He was saying it was a sin for one man to own another. Of course, people knew Mr. Minton was against slavery, but to preach about it — well, that was different. A sermon wasn't just a statement of a man's private belief. Brady had heard his father say this time and again. A sermon was supposed to be God's word. And there were people sitting in the church right now who were not going to appreciate Mr. Minton's claiming that God was lined up on the side against them. There were others who might share Mr. Minton's ideas but who were undoubtedly frowning to themselves and saying that politics didn't belong in the pulpit.

Brady glanced sideways at his mother. She was staring straight ahead, her eyes unblinking, her face like stone. Oh, why did his father have to do it? Brady asked himself. Just the other day he'd been so all-fired anxious to keep peace in the community, for petey's sakes, and now look what he was doing. Breaking the peace into smithereens, that's what. Brady could feel the ladies in the church, their fans forgotten, stealing glances at his mother to see how she, a native of Virginia, was taking this kind of talk. Some of the men were looking at Uncle Earl, likely wondering how this would affect his prospects at the election. Even Mr. Fergus, who was such a good friend, looked unhappy. Brady felt the perspiration trickling down the back of his neck. How could his father do such a thing? How could he?

Brady picked a spot on the floor between his knees and stared at it, wishing it would open into a hole and swallow him up. He remembered the story about what

119

happened once in the early days when the first church building had been hastily put together for the winter. Right in the middle of the sermon one Sunday the whole floor had given way. No one had been hurt, only shaken up, but church had been adjourned. Why couldn't that happen now? Brady thought.

Instead, Mr. Minton's voice went on and on, and it was a while before Brady became aware of how quiet the voice actually was. In comparison, say, to Mr. McKain's ranting against slavery, Brady's father was as calm as if he were baptizing a baby. As a matter of fact, when you listened carefully to the words, you understood that Mr. Minton was making a plea for reason and intelligence and patience in solving the slavery problem. He said you had to move slowly to keep one part of the country from being too badly hurt, but the point was, you had to move. There was no getting away from it, Mr. Minton said that slavery was a sin. He said that God had not created all white men equal; He had created *all* men equal.

When the sermon was finally over and benediction said, Brady lifted his head just enough to watch his father walk to the front door to greet the congregation. He knew then that the worst was still to come. What would his mother do when she unclenched her hands? Would she sweep out of the church past her husband, not speaking, her mouth set in that straight line she used whenever slavery was mentioned? And all the other folks whispering, nodding, and shaking their heads. What would they do? Oh, now was the time, Brady realized, for the floor to cave in if it was ever going to.

But the floor didn't cave in, and when Brady looked up, his mother had already left the pew. She was standing at the front of the church beside her husband, her head high, smiling, her hand outstretched to welcome folks. It was something Brady had never seen his mother do. Normally she walked out of the church just like any other member of the congregation. Brady hung at the back of the church, watching his mother, thinking he'd never seen her look as lovely as she did at this minute. All at once it didn't matter any longer what other people did. They could shake Mr. Minton's hand and congratulate him as some folks were doing, or they could deliberately walk by without speaking. At the moment Brady didn't care. But when Mrs. Williams and her children sailed past, their noses pointed sky-high as if they smelled something bad, Brady felt his face grow hot. His hands knotted into fists and he longed for some of the snow he'd been dreaming of in church. He'd pack a good hard snowball, that's what he'd do. Better yet, he wished he could meet Laban Williams at the North Pole. He knew what he'd do there, all right — a place like that where a person could make his spit count. Man alive, did he ever know! Ping, ping, he whispered to himself as he watched Laban climb into the buggy with his mother and drive off.

The last of the congregation had gone now. Brady, his father and mother and Uncle Earl were left standing in the doorway.

Mr. Minton sighed and turned slowly to his wife. He

put his hand on her arm. "I thank you, my dear, for what you have done."

Mrs. Minton stood for a moment quietly, looking into the elm-shaded graveyard behind the church. Then she covered her husband's hand with her own. Her eyes, that had been so stony at the beginning of the sermon, began to twinkle. "Well, Thaddeus, you've taken this step and I'm your wife. The rest of the world won't know that I interpret God's word a mite differently, but I expect you'll go on knowing it."

Mr. Minton threw back his head and laughed. The first real laugh in weeks. "You mean I haven't heard the last of Henry Clay?"

"I should say not."

"Well, there comes a time," Mr. Minton said, serious again, "when a man has to bear witness to what he believes." He turned to his brother Earl. "I felt it was time to speak as I did, no matter what the consequences."

Uncle Earl held out his hand. "You did the right thing, Thad. It was a fine sermon. I was proud."

As they walked toward their buggy, Brady wished he could think of something splendid to say to his father. He was ashamed of the embarrassment he had felt in church, but try as he might, he didn't seem able to shape anything into words. Finally as he stepped into the buggy beside his father, he cleared his throat. "Well," he said, "I'm glad of one thing. I'm glad Mr. Williams isn't my pa."

Chapter Ten

WHEN BRADY saw Mr. Fergus drive up to the house that afternoon, he never thought of its having anything to do with his father's sermon. Although Mr. Fergus was known to support slavery in a quiet way, he had said he would never argue about it with Mr. Minton. Brady couldn't imagine anything breaking up the friendship of these two men or anything keeping Mr. Fergus from making his weekly calls. Everyone in the family enjoyed these calls. As soon as Mr. Fergus turned his buggy into the driveway, he would toot a funny little horn and Mrs. Minton would smile and put a kettle on for tea. Mr. Fergus would come in the back door like one of the family and right away he'd start finding out what each one had been doing. He wasn't interested in just a routine, polite way. His was a *real* interest. He would go out in the garden with Mrs. Minton to see her roses. Or he would reach into his pocket and pull out a special book for Uncle Earl or a hair ribbon for Mary Dorcas. He would take time to become acquainted with each of Brady's squirrels — not just brush past them and say, "For land's sakes, who ever heard of pet squirrels?" the way other people did.

Today, however, Mr. Fergus didn't toot his horn when he arrived. When he walked into the kitchen, instead of sitting down at the kitchen table, he suggested that they go into the parlor.

"I'm here on a church matter," he said, looking as solemn as George Washington.

Bewildered, Brady followed his family into the parlor. He stood quietly in the doorway, hoping no one would send him away, and watched Mr. Fergus take his place in the center of the black mohair loveseat. He straightened out his coattails and placed his hat carefully on the seat beside him. His manner was grave and formal. The Mintons ranged before him — Mr. Minton, his brother Earl, and Mrs. Minton — each on a straight-backed chair, waiting. Even Great-Grandfather Hugh in his gold frame on the wall seemed to be waiting.

All at once Mr. Fergus leaned his head forward in his hands. "Oh, Thaddeus," he cried, "why did you do it? Why did you preach as you did?"

It was frightening to see a grown man's composure so shaken. Especially Mr. Fergus. For a moment all Brady could hear in the room was Mr. Parley Potter's clock clicking away on the mantelpiece. Mr. Fergus sat with his head bowed.

At last Mr. Minton spoke. "Well, Emmett," he said gently, "I didn't expect you to agree with everything I said but I thought you of all people would respect my reasons for speaking."

"Not in the pulpit, Thaddeus! Not in the pulpit! What you say any place else is a private matter. I wouldn't argue with you. What you say in the pulpit is a church matter."

"And there are some in the church who disapprove and have sent you to tell me so. Is that it?" Mr. Minton's voice was tired.

Mr. Fergus nodded unhappily. "This afternoon there was a meeting of some church members sympathetic to slavery. Bill Williams got himself elected chairman and proposed that whatever course of action we decided to take, we would take as a group. We agreed to act together in this way, even though there might be some dissension among us. There were several courses of action discussed." Mr. Fergus paused, then went on with difficulty. "I was asked to bring you the result."

125

"And what was the nature of this vote, Emmett?"

From an inside pocket Mr. Fergus took out a sheet of paper. He unfolded it, and slowly and painfully he read it aloud. "Resolved: that inasmuch as Mr. Minton's sermon on this third Sunday in July, 1836, was political, irreligious, and inflammatory, and inasmuch as the arguments propounded have no basis in the Bible, we, the undersigned, no longer wish to attend services of worship conducted by Mr. Minton. We intend in the future to conduct our own services separately at a time to be arranged when the church building is not otherwise in use."

Mr. Fergus handed the paper to Mr. Minton. Brady's mother and Uncle Earl sat as still as if they were in picture frames like Great-Grandfather Hugh.

"I see your name is down here, Emmett," Mr. Minton said finally.

"Yes. I tried to promote another course of action but I was outvoted. But you must know I hoped it wouldn't come to this."

"It was a moderate sermon, Emmett. I advocated reason and patience."

"You also said slavery was an evil. That it was against the dictates of God."

"And don't you believe that, Emmett?"

The two old friends faced each other miserably across the room. It was as if no one else was around.

"The Hebrews themselves had slaves, Thaddeus. I grant that there may be some abuse of slavery which is, indeed, an evil. But the cure for poor treatment is better treatment. Not freedom. Why, a slave doesn't have the capacity to use freedom, Thaddeus. It would be no kindness to give it to him."

"Bosh!" The word burst out of Mr. Minton before he was aware of it. Then in an effort to control himself, he paced back and forth across the narrow room, stopping at last in front of his friend.

"Emmett, Emmett," he said unhappily, "how can you believe that? In most Southern states it is against the law to teach a slave to read and write. Why? Because he doesn't have the capacity? No. It's because he *does* have the capacity. He learns and then he becomes restless for freedom."

Brady wished the conversation were taking place in the kitchen. His mother wouldn't be sitting so still if they were in the kitchen. She'd be walking around or bending over the stove all this while. Uncle Earl would be tilting his chair back against the wall, the way he liked to. And the clock wouldn't be ticking and Great-Grandfather Hugh smiling and smiling, so pleased with the world.

But Mr. Fergus was standing now, his hat in his hand. "It's a sad thing, Thaddeus, when a church splits over an issue that has no place in the church at all. Perhaps I could persuade Mr. Williams and the others to withdraw the petition if you would give some assurance that this subject won't be mentioned in the pulpit again."

"I couldn't do that, Emmett."

Mr. Fergus sighed. "No, I suppose not." Before going out the door, he turned back once again. "I'm sorry," he said simply.

The petition lay on the round-topped marble table in the center of the room. Uncle Earl picked it up. "Eighteen names," he said finally. "That's not many, Thaddeus. You've still got the major part of your congregation with you."

But Mr. Minton was already walking out of the room. Mrs. Minton, her face drawn with weariness, was going upstairs for a rest. Brady looked up at Great-Grandfather Hugh. "You don't know anything," he said under his breath. "I bet you never even heard of slavery."

Brady wished he hadn't heard of slavery either. One way or another slavery had just about changed everything. It had got him into trouble with his father, ruined his summer, upset his mother, was threatening Uncle Earl's job, and now it had divided the church. Brady sat on the back steps and watched his father walk slowly to the Sermon House. It was the first Sunday his father had forgotten to ask him to repeat the catechism. That showed how different things were now.

Although Brady supposed he was beginning to be against slavery too, it was hard to understand how a person could feel as strongly as his father did. As far as he knew, his father didn't know a single slave. Although there were still a few in Washington County, there weren't any nearby. How could you care so much what happened to slaves when you didn't even know any? Brady thought of the two slaves he'd seen at

Drover Hull's and, of course, he hoped they were safe
now and free. But how could you spend your days and
nights thinking about slavery when there was so much
right under your own nose to worry about?

Like your father not trusting you. Like being kept
on the farm all summer as if you were a five-year-old.
Like not wanting to go hunting.

Like knowing Laban Williams, for petey's sakes.
Laban had always been hard enough to bear, but what
would he be like now that his father had succeeded in
splitting the church in half? There would be no stopping Laban and his pa now. Likely they thought they
could run the town.

Still, the next morning when Brady saw the piece of
paper nailed to the barn, he didn't think of either Laban
or Bill Williams right away. The paper was a foot
square, planted right in the middle of the red barn door.
Even before Brady was close enough to read the paper,
he had a queer feeling about it.

> THE MINTONS ARE TOO DING CLOSE TO THE
> MASON DIXON LINE.
> GO ON NORTH WHERE YOU BELONG.

That's what the paper said. The writing was crude
and could have been written by anyone, but as far as
Brady was concerned, he knew who had done it. Just as
soon as he read it, he knew. Only Bill and Laban Williams could be so mean. Brady felt his face fire up as he

snatched down the paper, then swung around and held it out to his father and Uncle Earl, who were on their way to the barn. Uncle Earl was going to Washington for a couple of weeks.

Brady thrust the paper into his father's hand. "Just look at that!" he cried. "Just look what the Williamses have done now." Brady's chest was heaving the way it did when he ran up a long hill without stopping.

Mr. Minton read the note and handed it to his brother.

"I'm going to hit that Laban Williams," Brady panted. "When I see him, I'm going to punch him right between the eyes."

"You're going to do no such thing." Mr. Minton sounded as if he'd run up a short hill himself. "You can't prove the Williamses had anything to do with this. We don't know who did it. Could have been a dozen different people."

Uncle Earl nodded. "You start accusing anyone without proof and we'd really be in trouble." He read the note over again slowly. "I guess they think they can scare us out or else get us so mad we'll do something we shouldn't. Either way, they'd be rid of us."

"They'll have a hard time getting rid of me." The line on Mr. Minton's jaw was tight. He and his brother Earl turned toward the barn.

Brady followed. "You mean you're not going to do anything about this? Just let them say whatever they please? Uncle Earl is sheriff, for petey's sakes!"

"Well, I won't be sheriff long if I go around saying things I'm not able to prove," Uncle Earl said. "Nor if anyone else in this family does either." He had started to saddle his horse but stopped and turned to his brother. "The way things are, Thaddeus, maybe I shouldn't go to Washington."

"Oh no, Earl. You go ahead. They're just trying to scare us. Nothing you could do."

Mr. Minton put his hand out and took hold of Brady's shoulder.

"If you find any more papers like that around the farm, save them for me. And don't tell anyone about them. Not even Range."

"Yes, sir."

"And if you see Laban Williams, don't mention the papers. And for land's sakes, don't touch him."

Brady swallowed. "No, sir."

Mr. Minton's hold on Brady tightened. "And don't tell your mother about any of this. No need to upset her."

"I won't."

Still Mr. Minton didn't let go. "Are you sure you can keep quiet?"

"Yes." Brady whispered his answer. His father still didn't believe he could keep any kind of secret at all. After all this time.

As Brady went about the farm that day, he found three other papers nailed up here and there. Even without any evidence, a person would know the Williamses had done it, Brady thought, tearing down a note tacked to the fence by the cornfield.

GIT OUT, the note read. YER NOT WELCOME.

131

Brady felt his breath coming quick again. Who else would be so eager to get rid of the Mintons? With Earl Minton out of the way, Bill Williams would be elected sheriff easily.

Brady folded up the latest note and put it in his pocket with the others. There was one that had been nailed to a tree in the pasture. It had only one word on it, GIT. The worst one, however, had been tacked to the door of the woodshed. It was a rough-looking picture of a man with splattered lines sticking out all over him. TAR AND FEATHERS were the words written under it. Brady couldn't think of that picture without doubling his hand into a fist.

Brady's job that morning was to work the vegetable patch behind the barn. It was a small patch — potatoes, peas, beans, and a few rows of cabbages. As he kneeled down to pull up the weeds, he could feel the notes in his shirt pocket burning a hole, it seemed, right through to his skin. He picked up a stone embedded in the ground and threw it across the fields. When his father saw all these notes, surely he'd do something about them. At least he'd agree that Bill Williams had written them. Brady kept one eye on the door of the Sermon House. As soon as his father stepped out of that door, Brady would show him the notes.

From row to row Brady worked his way, in turn stooping over and then down on his hands and knees. "Git," he said, jerking up a weed, "yer not welcome." All the time the sun beat down on the vegetable patch

— hotter and hotter as if the day was working up to some kind of climax.

And, indeed, it seemed to be. Brady glanced up and saw thunderclouds forming in the west. In the lower pasture the two cows were already standing under the oak tree, and in the cornfield the scarecrow was flapping his arms. And then Mr. Minton stepped out of the Sermon House. He'd barely closed the door before Brady was calling and running to him.

Still standing before the door, Mr. Minton read the notes, one after another. When he had finished, he put them in his vest pocket. "I think I'll go into town and see Dr. Scott," he said quietly.

"You think you and Dr. Scott can stop Bill Williams?"

Mr. Minton and Brady were walking up the hill together. "Brady, I told you to forget about Bill Williams." Mr. Minton spoke sharply. "We don't know any more than we did before. I just think it would be a good idea for someone outside the family to see these notes in case anything further develops."

"Like what?" Brady matched his steps to his father's stride.

"Well, I don't anticipate anything. I'm sure this is aimed to scare us and that's all. But I want to talk to Dr. Scott." Mr. Minton turned into the barn. "Tell your mother I've gone into town, Brady. But don't tell her about the notes. Remember. Nor anyone else."

"I'll remember," Brady mumbled. "I already promised I wouldn't." He handed his father the saddle. Then

133

he took a deep breath. "May I go with you?" he asked.

Mr. Minton didn't even look up. "No. I want you to stay on the farm, Brady."

Brady slumped down against the barn door and watched his father ride off. He picked up a handful of pebbles and began peppering the ground with them. Then all at once he dropped the pebbles in a lump. There had been something strange about the way his father had left the Sermon House. Brady remembered his father coming out of the Sermon House and stopping to read the notes, but for the life of him he couldn't remember his father locking the door. Brady got slowly to his feet. He guessed he might as well go down and check that door himself.

Chapter Eleven

As many times as Brady had tried the Sermon House door when he had passed, it should have come natural to him. But now as he came near, he found himself hesitant to put his hand on the knob. He smiled at his foolishness, but as he reached out his hand a roll of thunder suddenly sounded behind him and Brady jumped back. For petey's sakes, he told himself. He grabbed the knob and pushed the door open.

It took a minute for his eyes to become adjusted to the dark room but then, as he looked around, Brady wondered why he had always been so curious. His father's desk was there, an old table, a faded rag rug, and a cot covered with a green and white quilt. There was nothing special about the room, nothing to justify all the mystery he'd built up in his mind. Disappointed, Brady sat down at his father's desk. Three partly used candles of differing heights rose above litters of papers and books. In the middle of the desk, Mr. Minton's Bible lay open.

"Seek ye Jehovah while he may be found," Brady read. "Call upon him while he is near."

Brady had always supposed that if he were to go into the Sermon House, he'd feel different. He'd supposed he would, in one way or another, have the feeling that God was there too, but the fact was he didn't feel a thing. He started to turn to another page in the Bible, but he pulled his hand back quickly. If anything at all were changed in the room, his father would be suspicious. He stuffed his hands into his pockets and stood up. He stepped over a pile of books on the floor and wandered to the table in the center of the room. A plate with one raisin cookie was on the table and a glass half filled with milk. Brady wondered if his father would remember that there was one cookie left from what had apparently been a plateful. He decided he might. Somehow Brady had never pictured his father thinking about food while he was in the Sermon House.

A few drops of rain spattered down on the roof and Brady figured he'd better go. He looked around the room once more and for the first time he noticed the wall at the far end of the room. Like the other walls, it was made of rough boards — but this one had a large map of the Holy Land hanging over it. Brady remembered his father showing him this map years ago before there was a Sermon House. Pa used to ask him to locate Jerusalem and Bethlehem and Nazareth. Brady walked over to the map. He put his finger out and touched it, trying to find the spot marked Jerusalem. As he did, part of the wall swung open, revealing a narrow compartment beyond it.

The compartment was not empty. Sitting on the floor was a colored boy. He held himself absolutely still and stared wordlessly at Brady and Brady stared back.

You couldn't hear anything in the Sermon House now except the pattering of rain and an occasional grumble of thunder. Brady leaned against the wall, his heart hammering. With part of his mind he noticed that the boy was not much older than he was, maybe about Range's age. The boy's eyes were round with fright. With another part of his mind Brady tried to digest all that this discovery meant. This boy was a runaway slave. His father was an underground agent. Brady formed the words slowly in his mind, one at a time, and then repeated them because they were so hard to believe. The Sermon House was a station.

The runaway boy finally broke the silence. "You alone?" he asked.

Brady nodded.

"You Mr. Minton's son?"

Brady nodded again. "My name's Brady," he whispered.

The boy didn't stir but the startled look was leaving his eyes.

"Your pa know you're here?"

Brady shook his head.

"Your pa ain't goin' to like it. Where's he at?"

Brady ran his tongue around his dry lips. "He went to town."

"Anyone else at your house likely to come bustin' in?"

"Only my mother's home. She won't come here." Brady put his hands in his pockets so the runaway boy wouldn't see how they were shaking.

"Your pa's not goin' to like your bein' here," the boy said again. "He's goin' to be madder'n a wet hen."

Brady swallowed hard. "Are you going to tell him?"

Instead of answering, the boy smiled. "You got anything to eat with you?"

Brady shook his head. "Should I get something?" he asked.

"Naw, it ain't necessary." The boy shrugged. "Better that you don't be runnin' in and out. I ain't really hungry anyway. Just wonderin', that's all. Sometimes folks carries a little something in their pockets."

Brady wished he could reach into his pocket and pull out a package with a piece of his mother's apple pie, but the only thing he had in his pockets were his own trembling hands.

"Your pa keeps me well enough supplied," the boy said. "I was finishin' some cookies and a glass of milk out there when I heard you callin' out. Guess it was you. Sent me scuttlin' through the Jerusalem door so fast, I forgot to put the catch on. Else you never would have found me."

"I'll get you your milk and cookie," Brady offered, turning back toward the big room. He took his hands out of his pockets and slowly wiped the perspiration from them onto the seat of his trousers. Then with a nervous glance at the Sermon House door, he carried the food back to the alcove.

The boy smiled. His long legs lay sprawled in front of him; his back was propped against the outer wall. He was so relaxed now, you wouldn't guess he was a runaway with Bill Williams and a lot of other folks willing to give their eyeteeth to get their hands on him.

"Long as you're here, Master Brady," the boy said softly, "can't you set down a spell and talk? Your pa's a fine man, but he ain't much of a talker, is he?"

Brady slid uneasily to the floor.

"My name's Moss," the boy said. He broke the raisin cookie and offered half of it to Brady.

Brady shook his head. "You eat it."

"Moss is the only name I got right now," the boy

139

went on, taking a swallow of milk. "But just you wait. Once I'm free, I'm goin' to hitch onto a name that'll be like a banner flyin' all my days."

"What name?"

Moss looked off into space. "Don't rightly know yet," he said. "But it'll be one I can take pride in." He took a bite of cookie, then looked at the remaining portion still in his hands. "You like animals?" he asked suddenly.

Brady nodded and as he followed Moss' eyes, he noticed for the first time a little makeshift cage in the corner of the alcove. Moss leaned over and pulled it toward him. Peeking out of the cage was a small gray field mouse.

"I call him Lisha," Moss said. He held the piece of cookie out to the mouse. "Come on, little man," he whispered. His voice was a kind of gentle cooing. "Mind your manners now, hear? We got us some company."

Brady leaned forward tensely and watched the mouse scuttle around Moss' fingers, his whiskers twitching.

"You got no cause to be bashful," Moss coaxed. "You ben eatin' off my fingers for three days now. Why you hangin' back?" When the mouse still held back, Moss pushed his fingers in farther.

In spite of his nervousness, Brady couldn't help grinning. "Where did you get him?"

"Oh, he just marched hisself in here, bold as brass, the first night I came and we made friends," Moss explained. "Your pa let me rig up a little cage for him so's he could keep me company."

Brady put his finger in the cage and touched the soft fur. Then all at once he found himself telling Moss about Catfish and the squirrels. He talked quickly, still in a whisper, squatting on his heels, ready to jump at the first sound.

Moss' eyes sparkled. "Sure wish I could see those squirrels," he said. "It gets mightly lonesome here sometimes."

"How long have you been here?" Suddenly questions were tumbling over themselves and Brady couldn't ask them fast enough.

"Mr. Parley Potter brought me here the night of Fourth of July," Moss said. "He's the one does the travelin' in the South and brings the slaves, one or two at a time, over the border. We followed that ol' North Star, like Mr. Potter said, and it brought us right here to your pa's."

"How long are you going to be here?"

Moss scratched his head. "I forget just when your pa said he's gonna take me north. He's goin' to leave me with another agent who's to take some of us young runaways to a school in Canada. I'm goin' to get me some learnin'." He laughed. "Me and my double-bar-reled name, whatever it turns out to be."

Some of the pieces began to fit together now in a puzzle that Brady had not even been aware existed. Uncle Will's place must be the next station north. His father was likely planning to deliver Moss on the same trip that he picked up Mary Dorcas. And Mr. Parley Potter was in on the whole thing, for petey's sakes! Brady remembered his father and Uncle Will and Mr. Potter walking over the hill, talking together.

"Did Mr. Potter ever try to teach you any mental arithmetic?" he asked.

"Lordy!" Moss laughed. "He didn't give me no peace at all."

Brady and Moss grinned at each other and listened to the wind blowing up outside. A sudden clash of thunder brought the rain pounding down on the Sermon House. A tree branch scratched against the roof.

Brady started up. "I've got to go." How long had he been here anyway? Lightning, flashing through the window of the Sermon House and the open Jerusalem door, was sending great jagged streaks into the narrow alcove. With each fresh streak of light Brady became more aware not only of the danger that he was in with his father but the bigger, terrible danger they were all in together. His father, Uncle Earl, himself. All of them and more too when you thought about it. His Uncle Will and Mr. Potter and people he didn't even know. On and on. Moss too, perhaps more than anyone else. Brady looked over at Moss holding the mouse in his two hands, soothing him through the storm. The whole business of slavery was suddenly so enormous, Brady couldn't let himself think about it. "I've got to go," he said and stood up.

Moss stood up too. "Think you can ever come again?" he asked.

The whole room was blinking on and off now in the lightning. Brady didn't answer.

Moss ran a finger down the mouse's back. "If it's ever safe," he said, "and you get the chance, just you rap on the wall here three times and I'll answer you with three raps. Then I'll let you in."

Brady nodded. Then as he started to step out of the Jerusalem door, Moss called him back.

"I reckon you know," he said, "I'll never let on to your pa."

Brady looked at the tall, lanky boy, still cradling the mouse. He waited for a roll of thunder to subside.

"Guess you know too," Brady said, "I'll never tell." He reached out and touched the mouse. "And I'll try and come back."

Chapter Twelve

Brady was sure that all his father had to do was to
take one look at him and he'd know what had happened. How could anyone keep a piece of knowledge
such as Brady had from showing in his face, or for that
matter, from slipping out of his mouth, no matter how
careful he tried to be? At supper that night Brady didn't
know where to look or what to say. There were just

the three of them at the kitchen table — his mother and his father and himself, so close together it didn't seem possible one could hide a secret from the others. And yet this was just what his father had been doing day after day, Brady suddenly realized. He glanced up at his father, at his weary face, at the crease between his eyes, and the full burden of his father's secret swept over him. His father was an agent in the Underground Railroad! Not only that, the slavery folks were trying to run him out of the county. The notes seemed even more dangerous now that Brady knew about the Underground Railroad. As a matter of fact, there seemed to be danger in any direction he looked, and for the first time Brady was able to see it from his father's viewpoint. Of course his father couldn't take chances with a talkative son! Brady wished he could lean across the table, touch his father's arm, and tell him he understood. But that was the very thing he must never do.

In fact, that was the trouble. He couldn't speak his mind at all. Everything that happened seemed to have new meaning, and Brady didn't know how he could keep back an unwary comment or a knowledgeable look. Out of the corner of his eye he watched his father filling his plate, piling it high with an unusual amount of food. Then his father asked to be excused. He'd like to take his plate and eat in the Sermon House, he said, while he made some notes. Brady realized that the food was going to Moss. He wished he could slip another biscuit onto the plate and something for Lisha. Some raisins, perhaps. There were plenty of raisins in the pantry. He knew right where they were, on the second shelf. Then Brady caught himself. In another minute, the way his mind was working, he might have gone into the pantry. It wasn't even safe for him to think, it appeared, yet he didn't know how to stop.

If it was difficult for Brady to keep his knowledge of the secret from his mother and father, it was even harder to keep it from Range. The next day, when Range came up with his gun, suggesting that they go after blackbirds on the Minton place, Brady was sure the secret must stick out all over him. Try as he might, he couldn't keep his mind away from the Sermon House. As the boys walked toward the cornfield, Brady was too distracted even to pretend that he enjoyed hunting. In fact, he didn't talk at all. When Range brought down his first two blackbirds on the wing, Brady didn't comment or seem to notice how good the shots were. Instead, he was looking around to see if there were any new notes put up overnight. And he was wondering how he was going to see Moss again.

"Let's see you do as well," Range said, firing again and bringing down another bird.

They were at the cornfield and the scarecrow, not much higher than the corn now, stared at them.

"Well, what are you waitin' for?" Range snapped, annoyed at Brady's indifference. "Waitin' for a bird to hold still?"

Actually there weren't many birds in the cornfield, but there was one that had just alighted, brazen as you please, right on the scarecrow's head. Range pointed to him.

"He's askin' for it," he said. "You couldn't have a better target if you set it up. Dare you to get him."

Brady raised his rifle, sighted, and pulled the trigger — but instead of dropping to the ground the bird spiraled into the air, and Drover Hull's scarecrow head fell forward into the cornstalks. It hung dangling by its white yarn, its eyes goggling at Brady. Brady shivered. He felt the same as he had when Drover Hull had spit that tobacco juice in his direction.

Range was disgusted. He walked over and put the scarecrow head back on the body, but now it listed crazily to one side, its eyes gazing up in a way that was more spooky than ever. No matter how Range jiggled it, he couldn't straighten the angle of the head. He turned back to Brady, who stood with his arms hanging like sticks at his sides, his mind far away.

"What's ailing you today anyhow?" Range grumbled. "You been woolgatherin' all morning. Ain't no fun at all bein' with you. You might as well go home as act like that." He humped himself around and started toward the lower end of the field.

Brady followed slowly, watching Range's light, quick figure ahead. Now look what he'd done, Brady said to himself. On top of everything else, he'd made Range mad, and if there was anything Brady hated, it was that unsettled feeling of being on the outs with Range Hadley. Well, maybe if he shot down a whole mess of blackbirds, he could straighten things out.

But then he thought of a better way. He could tell Range his secret. Never had he kept a secret from Range before, and of course that was probably his trouble now, the very reason why he couldn't act natural. It was a pretty lonely kind of business, hiding something from your best friend. Besides, Brady reasoned, if he told Range, it wouldn't be the same as if he told anyone else. Range had been in on their Underground discoveries right from the start. Telling him wouldn't be so much breaking a secret as it would be simply keeping him abreast of developments. Brady quickened his steps and began to think that maybe he really *should* tell Range. Having Range to talk to would in a way almost ensure the secret. He was so afraid he was going to let something slip when he was with his father or his Uncle Earl or even someone outside the family, but if he could speak freely to just one person, such as Range, the pressure would lessen. He wouldn't be nearly as likely to talk out of turn with other folks. Besides, hadn't his father told Dr. Scott about the notes? This wouldn't be any different.

"If you don't want to shoot, why don't you say so?" Range called crossly over his shoulder.

"Sure, I want to." Brady went on with his thoughts. Range was so closemouthed, the secret would be as safe as if it were buried.

"You ain't even tryin'," Range growled. "You're just stumblin' along, bein' quiet and queer, not payin' attention to anything. I'd have a better time if I was with Laban Williams."

Brady felt his cheeks burn. If Range only knew! He was leading the way now down into the swampy part of the hollow where, Brady knew, red-winged blackbirds would be hanging onto the reeds as if they grew there, part of the plants themselves. With every step Brady felt his secret growing bigger and bigger inside him. Pretty soon it would have to break out; he wouldn't be able to help himself. When they got down to the hollow, he'd tell — all about Moss and his mouse and the Jerusalem door, all about the notes Bill Williams had put up the day before. He pictured how Range would grin and let out a long whistle of surprise. "No wonder," he'd say, "you couldn't keep your mind on the pesky blackbirds." Then they'd talk and speculate together.

But when they got down to the hollow, Range in his unpredictable way changed his mind about shooting.

"Let's go into the woods," he said. "We haven't been over to Drover Hull's place since that day with the slave catcher. I have a notion how we can get into the cabin. For all we know, we might find Drover's corpse in there. We don't have any real reason to think different."

Brady looked at his friend miserably. "I can't," he said. "You know I can't. Pa says I'm not to go off the farm."

Range sat down, straddling an old stump. "So?" he asked. "He'll never know the difference."

It was true. His father was on another part of the farm, but still Brady didn't want to go. When he went off the farm the first time after his punishment, somehow he didn't want to sneak off.

"You done plenty of things your pa don't know

about, Brady Minton," Range said. "What's got into you?"

That was true enough too. But for some reason Brady just didn't want to. His father had enough trouble without being deceived any more. Besides, the secret Brady had stumbled upon was no little boy's secret and he didn't want to go running off like a little boy. Range would understand as soon as he told him.

"No," Brady said. "I don't want to. You won't either once I tell you something."

Range had raised his rifle again. "I'll bet you're just scared of looking at a corpse."

Brady shook his head. "That's not it. You just listen to the reason."

But Brady didn't have a chance to say any more. Range pulled his trigger at a flash of wings in the sky and a redbird fell to the ground.

Brady drew in his breath. "It's a redbird!" he cried. "Range Hadley, why don't you look what you're doing! You've shot a redbird."

Range didn't move from his stump. There was no way to tell whether he felt bad or not. There never was with Range. Brady picked up the lifeless red body while the blackbirds, frightened by the shot, circled screaming overhead.

Range stood up and gave his trousers a hitch. "Well," he said, "I reckon a bird's a bird."

Brady swallowed. "I reckon." He put the redbird down, pushing it under a clump of moss he loosened near the tree stump.

Range started for the woods. "You comin' or not?" he asked.

"I guess not."

Brady watched Range disappear among the trees. Then slowly he started up the hill while the blackbirds drifted like leaves back to their stems. He hadn't told the secret after all. The secret was still inside him, big as ever, unshared, but somehow quiet now. Brady looked at the Sermon House standing high on the hill above him. He walked toward it, but it seemed to him the hill had never been so steep. When he finally reached the house, he had to stop for breath. What had he been thinking of anyway? he asked himself. Why, he'd actually persuaded himself with the crookedest kind of reasons, he realized now, that it would be all right to tell. Brady leaned against the side of the Sermon House, surprised to find that he was panting. Keeping a secret like this one was like riding a runaway horse. You didn't dare let go for a minute, he thought, and even then you didn't know where you would end up.

Chapter Thirteen

For the rest of that week things were so quiet that a person would never suspect that there was anything out of the ordinary going on at the Minton farm. Even Bill Williams seemed to be holding his peace. No new notes appeared. An outsider observing the Mintons on their way to church the next Sunday, the first Sunday since Mr. Fergus' visit, would have seen nothing exceptional — a preacher dressed in black driving a buggy; beside him, his wife, her worried expression hidden by a bonnet; and in the back seat a lanky boy no more restless than a boy is apt to be on the Sabbath. Moreover, the service itself was no different from other services of worship. The sermon was about the importance of observing the Sabbath; the congregation was attentive and grave. Although there were some pews empty, an outsider would scarcely have attached any significance to that. Nor after the service would he have imagined anything uncommon in the sight of a boy jumping out from behind a gravestone to make a face at the preacher's son. Indeed, even had he seen the restraining hand of the preacher on his son's arm or heard mutterings about a boy called Laban Williams, he would not have dreamed that behind this boyish scene, behind the empty pews, behind the gravity of the congregation, lay one issue, pulling and tearing at the community. Slavery.

On the surface, life went on in such a normal way that Brady had to pinch himself sometimes to remember the danger they were all in. But at other times the sense of danger swept over him in a rush. Perhaps he'd see a notice of a runaway slave in the Washington newspaper that came to his father once a week. Or he'd read about the abolitionist preacher, Moses Lowe, getting into trouble again. Or then he might look in the direction of the cornfield and see the scarecrow's head wobbling to one side and he would be reminded of Drover Hull. Maybe Drover really was dead inside his

cabin as Range had suggested. Bill Williams or someone with his sentiments might easily have killed him.
It was the kind of thing that could happen to a person
running an Underground Railroad station.

Threading in and out of all the other thoughts, however, was the thought of Moss. It was with Brady con-
stantly. As he went about his chores — weeding the
vegetable patch, chopping wood, feeding the chickens,
milking the cows — he imagined Moss cramped in his
dark corner, the long hours dragging slowly by one
after another and nothing to do but talk to a field
mouse. Moss was likely listening and listening for those
three taps on his wall, wondering why Brady didn't
come back. But Brady had determined that no matter
how much he wanted to see Moss, he wasn't going to
get himself or anyone else into more trouble. Brady
wasn't going to risk tapping on the wall unless it was
really safe. Unless there was no one on the farm and no
one coming up the road from either direction.

Then four days before Mr. Minton was to go for
Mary Dorcas, Brady's chance came. At breakfast Mr.
Minton said that he was going to call on some folks in
town and see if he couldn't round up several barrels of
old clothes to take with him when he went for Mary
Dorcas. His brother Will had spoken about a Negro
school in Canada that was in need of clothing, he said
in a tone so casual you would never have guessed there
was a runaway slave hiding on his farm that very minute whom he planned to take along with those clothes.
Brady busied himself with his breakfast. He was piling

hot cakes one on top of another when he heard his mother say that she thought she'd go along with Mr. Minton and take some of her new preserves to Mrs. Scott. All at once Brady realized that he was going to be alone. He took a big bite of hot cakes so he wouldn't be tempted to smile.

The first thing Brady did when his mother and father had gone was to climb up to the third floor and look out the storeroom window. It was a tiny window tucked under the peak of the roof and when he looked out, he saw a different world from the one he knew on the ground. When he'd been a little boy, Brady had stood on a stool to look out the window and every time he'd been freshly surprised at how strange everything seemed. The barn, that was so enormous when you stood in it, looked from the storeroom like a cardboard building that you could pick up in your hand if you had a mind to. And the road to town became a narrow ribbon laid smoothly across the hills.

It was the road that interested Brady today. He leaned far out the window and studied the whole ribbonlike length. A person coming up either side of the Minton hill would be seen quickly enough from here. Brady spotted his father's buggy, so reduced in size now it was hard to believe anyone was sitting in it. He waited while the buggy moved farther and farther toward town until, he figured, it was too late for his mother or father to say they had forgotten something at home and they'd better turn around and get it. There was no one coming up the road from either side. As a matter of fact, there was no sign of life except a few miniature cows scattered here and there on the hillsides. Even if a stranger should appear on the road now, it would be twenty minutes or more before he could reach the house.

Brady hurried downstairs to the kitchen, made a chicken sandwich, cut a piece of apple pie, and gathered up a handful of raisins. As he went outside, he caught sight of the smallest of Catfish's adopted squirrels working on an old apple core under the steps. It was the only squirrel left; the rest had gone back to the woods.

"You come too." Brady grinned, scooping the squirrel upon his shoulder. "Guess you won't tell any tales."

At the back of the Sermon House Brady tapped three times on the wall. He smiled, imagining how pleased Moss would be to hear the signal, but strangely enough, there was no immediate answer. Brady tried again, waited a minute, then went around to the door. It was locked. Then as he stood, uncertain what to do next, he had a terrible thought. Perhaps Moss had already gone. Brady had just guessed that his father would take Moss with him when he went for Mary Dorcas. Maybe that wasn't the plan at all.

Brady put the squirrel under his arm and rushed to the back of the Sermon House. He tapped again — louder this time, three insistent knocks. Then while he held his breath, the answer came — one, two, three. In a flash Brady was at the door, ready to slip in the moment it opened.

Moss chuckled. "Hey! You brought your squirrel!" His face lighted up with pleasure, as Brady had known it would.

Brady leaned against the door. It was so good to know that Moss was still here that for a moment all Brady could do was smile.

"Dinged if you ain't a cute rascal," Moss murmured as he squatted down to make friends with the squirrel. "I didn't think I'd get a chance to meet you."

"I didn't think so either," Brady said. "Where were you? I knocked before and you didn't answer."

Moss looked up surprised. "I didn't hear you 'cept that once. Reckon I must have been asleep. I spend a lot of time sleepin'." He held out a finger for the squirrel to investigate, then watched with delight as the squirrel went around the room, sniffing at walls, nosing into corners. But when the squirrel jumped up on the table, Brady reached for him.

"Maybe I better put him out," he said nervously. "He might disturb something."

"Oh, don't put him out yet, Master Brady," Moss pleaded. "He's not goin' to do anything I can't straighten out before your pa gets here."

The squirrel was on the couch now. Moss went over and started stroking him and with one hand began shaping a corner of the green and white quilt into a round nestlike place. Before Brady realized what Moss was up to, the squirrel had settled down in the nest as quiet as you please.

"He'll likely go to sleep in a minute or so," Moss explained. "In a dark room like this a squirrel would just as soon sleep, once he gets the notion."

Brady watched in amazement as the squirrel blinked his eyes and did, indeed, seem to be settling down for sleep. "How do you know so much about animals?"

"I've gentled quite a few," Moss explained. "All kinds. It ain't so hard. Animals has a lot of the same feelin's folks do. Look at that squirrel now." The squirrel had pushed his head deep under his bushy tail. "Give me a nest in a dark room," Moss went on, "and I do the same thing. That's why I didn't hear you the first time you knocked."

"I brought you something." Now that the squirrel had quieted down, Brady held out the package of food, grinning at Moss' pleasure, particularly when he discovered the raisins.

"Lisha's goin' to be your friend for life," Moss chuckled. "After I leave and he's set free, likely he'll dog your footsteps, lookin' for raisins."

They moved into the Jerusalem room.

"Guess you'll be leaving soon," Brady said when they had settled down on the floor.

Moss was eating his sandwich and pushing one raisin at a time in through the bars of the cage. "Four more days," Moss said. "Your pa's goin' to leave me at his brother's. Some man's goin' to take us runaways across a lake so big you can't even see the other side. And I never been on water before!" Moss shook his head at the thought of it. "Your pa says we gotta make sure to be at his brother's on time or I'll miss out. They'd have to go right on without me." Moss paused a moment. When he spoke again, his voice was a whisper. "I'm goin' to get to Canada all right, ain't I? You think so, don't you, Master Brady? You think I'll be all right, don't you?"

Moss' fear was like a cold draft seeping into the alcove. Brady shivered. "Of course you are," he said loudly. "Before you know it, you'll be walking around a freeman with two names."

Moss smiled. "I hope you're right, Master Brady. About the name, too. Only thing is, I can't think of a name that suits. Maybe you could tell me some since you been to school and all." He took a bite of sandwich.

Brady tried to go over some of the names in the Bible and in his history book, but instead of names, all he seemed able to see was pictures. Pictures of Moss on a strange street, Moss in a boat with waves so high you couldn't see over them. Moss hiding somewhere, somehow, in the back of his father's buggy.

"If you could just name me a good strong name, Master Brady," Moss urged.

Again Brady tried, but new pictures crowded into the dim alcove — pictures of slave catchers and men with mean eyes like Bill Williams, and Moss alone and needing help. All at once he felt himself bursting with a man-sized ability to help, to do something important. More than just bringing Moss a piece of apple pie, for petey's sakes!

"I can't think of a name now," Brady admitted at last.

Then suddenly there was no time for thinking or talking either. A faint whistle from the lower fields drifted into the Sermon House and Brady was on his feet. That was Range's whistle.

Brady went into the other room and carefully pulled back a corner of the curtain from the window. There was Range, who hadn't been around since the day he killed the redbird, walking up the hill and whistling for Brady. He was starting around the other side of the barn on the way to the house. In a minute he'd be knocking on the back door and there would be no answer. Then likely he'd go hello-ing into the barn and around the cornfield. Brady let the curtain fall back into place. It was going to be mighty hard to explain where he'd been, especially if the subject happened to come up in the presence of his father.

Brady looked at Moss, who had followed him into the big room, his eyes round and watchful, a piece of apple pie still in his hand.

"I better go," Brady whispered. He peeked out the window again. Now was the time, quickly, while Range was on the other side of the barn and wouldn't see him slipping out.

Brady looked helplessly at Moss. "It seems as if I just got here," he said. "And you haven't finished your pie." Then Brady was outside and the Sermon House door was closed behind him.

He walked quickly toward the house. He hadn't even said good-by to Moss. He hadn't wished him well or said any of the things he'd meant to. He pushed his hands impatiently into his pockets as he heard Range whistling again from the other side of the barn. Maybe Range had only come to borrow something. Maybe he'd leave in a few minutes, Brady thought, and there'd still be time to go back to the Sermon House.

But Range did not want to borrow anything. "Want to watch me make a box kite?" he asked, turning around on the back steps of the Minton house as Brady approached. "Can't work on it at home 'cause Pa don't want me to use up the string. I had to sneak it out. Come on." His hands were full of sticks, twigs, newspaper and string, and already he was leading the way to the shady side of the barn where he sat down and spread out his materials.

Brady sat down slowly, noting as he did that they were in full view of the Sermon House. A box kite, he muttered to himself. A box kite, for petey's sakes. This morning of all times. He looked up at the sky.

"Doesn't seem like kite weather to me," he said in what he hoped was a discouraging tone. "Not much breeze blowing."

Range had his knife out and was shaving a long, stout twig. "By the time I get this thing made, there may be a hurricane astir."

Brady sighed. "What's your pa doing?"

"Workin' on some contraption or other."

"What time do you have to be home?"

"No special time."

Brady tried again. "I have some chores to do pretty soon."

"Go ahead." Range was working deliberately, making his twigs into the thinnest, lightest sticks possible. "I'll stay here."

Brady leaned his back against the barn. Range was here for the morning, all right, and he might as well make the best of it. He stretched his legs out in front of him and tried to quiet his disappointment by letting his eyes wander over the fields almost ready now for harvest. In several weeks the corn would be gathered all over the countryside, the hay stacked, the fields flat again. And before long school would start.

"You going to school this year, Range?" he asked.

Range balanced the stick he'd been shaving on the end of a finger to test its weight. "I dunno. Maybe on and off."

The thought of school made Brady feel restless and impatient. Oh, he liked school well enough, he supposed, but there were days when he wished he could *do* something besides just getting ready and waiting to be a man. He'd felt the same way in the Sermon House when he'd wanted to help Moss. Sometimes life swelled up so big inside of him, it was hard to wait around and work sums and do chores. Brady stood up and kicked his toe into the dirt.

"Quit that," Range protested. "That dirt's goin' on my kite paper."

Brady threw himself back on the ground. "What are you going to do when you grow up, Range?" he asked.

Range measured the stick he was working on against

162

the one he'd finished. "Nothin' different from what I'm doin' now, I reckon," he said. "How about you?"

Brady rolled over on his back and stared into the blue sky.

"You goin' to be a teacher like your brother Matt?" Range asked.

"I don't know."

"Maybe you're thinkin' about being a preacher." Range spoke over a mouthful of string.

But Brady shook his head. "I just know one thing for sure," he said slowly. "When I grow up, I want to help get rid of slavery some way."

Range took the string out of his mouth. "Last time I heard, you hadn't made up your mind about slavery."

"Who said?" Brady sat up, startled. "Of course I'm against slavery."

Range rubbed his fingers down his twig to feel its smoothness. "The way I heard it, you weren't takin' sides."

Brady recalled the conversation with Range the day they had found Drover Hull's Underground station. It seemed a long time ago.

"Well, for petey's sakes," Brady exclaimed. "I'm talking about *now*. You think it's wrong now too, don't you?"

"I ain't wastin' my time thinkin'," Range said. "I don't care one way or another. It's no skin off my back."

Range leaned over his kite. How could Range not care, Brady thought impatiently — Range who always understood so much more and did things so much better than he did. Of course there were a lot of things Range didn't care about. Range was different from most folks, but up to now Range had generally seemed to be right and other folks wrong. Range's hands moved expertly among the kite materials, tying sticks together to form a frame. Watching him, Brady felt his irritation rise. It was all he could do to keep from telling Range Hadley a thing or two about slavery. But Brady knew that he'd better not get started, lest in spite of himself the secret slipped out.

He turned his attention away from Range and looked over at the Sermon House, sitting innocently under its elm tree as if it had grown there. Stalks of goldenrod stood on either side of the door, and under a corner of the roof a phoebe bird had built her nest. No one would suspect what the Sermon House really was. Even from the inside it looked innocent — a preacher's study and that was all. Moss would be behind the Jerusalem door now. Likely he'd be asleep, Brady figured, recalling how Moss said he spent much of his time that way. Then all at once Brady turned cold. Moss would not be the only one asleep. The squirrel was still in there on the couch!

For a moment all Brady could do was to stare stupidly at the locked door of the Sermon House, picturing his father's face when he discovered the squirrel. Brady's mind whirled with impossible schemes for getting into the Sermon House. He looked back at Range, still intent on that fool kite. He'd never known Range to stick to an idea for so long. Brady took a deep breath.

"You must be getting kind of sick of working on that kite, aren't you?" he began experimentally.

Range shrugged. "Nothin' much else to do."

"Why don't we go after blackberries?" If he could take Range away even for a few minutes, Brady figured, he'd find an excuse to slip back and get the squirrel.

"I don't feel like blackberryin'."

"Well, I'm tired of sitting here. How about going out to the road? There's a hole from the last rainstorm I'm supposed to fill in." He stood up as though he were ready to start.

"Go on if you want to," Range said. "I'm stayin'."

Brady sat down. In a moment he tried again. "Did you ever go to Drover Hull's cabin that day?"

"Never did." Range bit off a piece of string.

"I bet a person could get a reward for finding a corpse in an abandoned cabin like that. Especially if he could expose the criminal."

"Think so?"

"Sure. I've heard Uncle Earl talk about cases. If you went over now and discovered something, Pa would surely ask you to ride to Washington and tell Uncle Earl. Likely he'd lend you a horse."

"I dunno."

Brady glanced up at the sun. It was almost noon. Another few minutes or so and it might be too late.

Range held up the half-finished kite. "I'm goin' to finish this kite," he said.

Brady was desperate. "You hungry?" It was the last suggestion he could think of.

Range didn't look up. "Why?"

"There's some apple pie in the kitchen," Brady said without much hope. "I thought we could go and have a piece."

Range pushed his kite materials into a single pile. "Might as well," he agreed.

Such a simple thing. Why hadn't he thought of it before? In the kitchen Brady cut two large pieces of pie and put them on the table.

"Say," he said as Range sat down, "how about some cold buttermilk to go with that?" Already he was half-way to the door. "I'll just run down to the springhouse and bring back a pitcherful. You go on and start."

Brady let himself quickly out the back door, pre-pared to make a dash for the Sermon House, but he didn't get any farther. Coming up the road — indeed, turning in the driveway at that very moment — was his father's buggy. Brady sat down on the back steps. It was too late. His father would find the squirrel and dis-cover that Brady had been in the Sermon House. Brady's hand dangled loosely over the side of the steps as he watched his father drive up to the buggy shed. Maybe the best thing he could do, Brady decided, was to run away from home.

He felt something cold nuzzle into his hand. "Hello, Catfish," he said absent-mindedly without looking down. If he ran away, his father would probably be relieved too. At least then his father would be able to conduct his Underground station without a nosy boy around to bungle things up. "Isn't that right?" Brady asked and looked down at Catfish for confirmation.

Only it wasn't Catfish. It was the squirrel.

"For petey's sakes," Brady breathed. "Where did you come from?"

There was only one way the squirrel could have got out. Moss must have been watching from behind the curtain and when he saw Brady and Range go into the house, he'd put the squirrel out like a shot.

Brady grinned. He stuck his head back in the kitchen.

"Hey, Range," he called, "I think maybe there's a breeze blowing up so we can fly that kite of yours after all."

Chapter Fourteen

EVER SINCE Brady had first met Moss, he'd wondered how his father was going to take a runaway slave to Uncle Will's. Brady had heard stories about slaves wearing heavy veils and being disguised as women or else being hidden in a wagon full of chicken crates, but it didn't seem likely that Mr. Minton would pick either of these ways to hide Moss. The worst of it was that

Brady might never know how his father managed. Mr. Minton might slip away with Moss in the early morning while it was still dark, before anyone was stirring. If his father did that, Brady wouldn't be at the back doorstep, the way he planned, calling out a final good-by which Moss, hiding somewhere in the buggy or cart, would hear. "And good luck!" Brady would shout and Moss would know the good luck was meant for him. Brady guessed he'd always be disappointed that he hadn't had a chance to say a proper good-by to Moss or give him a keepsake of any kind. He might at least have done that. He didn't know what it would have been but something Moss could have kept for always. Something to bring him luck and to remind him of Brady and Lisha and the Sermon House.

As the day for Moss to leave came closer, Brady became more and more nervous. There was no reason to think anything would go wrong, and even if it did, Brady couldn't do much about it. So there was no sense in worrying. Still Brady did worry. He found himself jumping at sudden noises, looking over his shoulder for no reason at all. All summer, events had been building up and building up and he couldn't shake himself free of the idea that something was going to happen. It was like the minute hand on Mr. Potter's clock. It could go on ticking away the minutes for just so long and then it would have to strike. All the way around the circle of the clock that hand would build up the minutes irrevocably until it reached the top again. It would tremble there for a moment; then it would strike. Sometimes lying awake in bed at night, Brady would hear the clock give its little preliminary grumble and he would hold his breath until the striking was over. Now, two days before Moss was to leave, Brady found himself waiting, holding his breath sometimes almost as if he expected a clock to strike.

Brady wasn't anywhere near a clock, however, when the stranger came. Brady was working on the road, fixing the holes the rain had made. It was dusk; the evening meal was over when he straightened up from his job. And there was the stranger standing beside him, appeared from nowhere it seemed — a short, hawklike man with a dirty bandage around his head and a crest of black hair that rose straight up in the air.

"You live in that house?" the man asked, pointing with his chin to the Minton place.

"Yes, sir."

The man carried a Bible and a black hat in one hand and a shabby canvas valise in the other. Somehow he didn't look like a regular traveler nor like a tramp either.

"Your folks for or against?" He pointed with his chin again.

When Brady looked puzzled, the man raised his voice shrilly. "For or against slavery, of course! What else would you be for or against?"

Brady swung his shovel over his shoulder and decided he didn't like this man. "We're against slavery," he said shortly.

The stranger smiled, showing an uneven row of ragged teeth. "Then I'll stop here for my dinner." Immediately he turned toward the house. "Love ye therefore the sojourner," he recited loudly as he walked, "for ye were sojourners in the land of Egypt."

Travelers often stopped at the Minton house for a drink of water or for a rest, but if they needed a meal, they generally waited until it was offered. They didn't quote the Bible to you either — about loving sojourners, for petey's sakes. Brady found himself resenting this arrogant little man more and more. Who did he think he was anyway?

"You going far?" Brady asked.

The man threw back his head and the crest of his hair flopped down over his bandage. "Down into Egypt land, that's where I'm going," he cried.

The man must be daft, Brady thought. He opened the door and followed the stranger into the kitchen.

"I have heard the groaning of the people of Israel," the stranger announced, "and I have remembered my covenant."

That was the way the stranger introduced himself to Mr. and Mrs. Minton, but in a moment he was explaining that he had a long trip ahead and he'd like some food. When he was talking about food, Brady noticed, the stranger made himself perfectly clear and left the Bible out of it. "No cheese," he said. "Cheese doesn't set well with me."

Well, for petey's sakes, Brady muttered again.

"My name's Lowe," the man said. "I'll give you my card." He stooped down to open his valise. When he stood up again, he had a handful of small printed cards.

He gave some to Mr. Minton and put the rest on the table.

Brady reached over for one.

MOSES LOWE
PREACHER FOR FREEDOM
"I will smite with the rod."

That's what the card said. Moses Lowe! The abolitionist preacher. The man that folks threw eggs at!

"Yes, I'm Moses Lowe," the man said. "Come to deliver the slaves from their bondage. I expect you've heard of me."

There was a complete silence in the kitchen; then Mrs. Minton slammed down a teakettle on the kitchen stove. The noise of the teakettle was as sudden and sharp as if a clock had struck the first note of midnight. Brady sucked in his breath.

That moment was the beginning. Afterward when Brady thought over the breathless events that followed, it always seemed to him that they had been triggered off by that strange man standing in the kitchen and saying *"I'm Moses Lowe."* At first Brady had thought only about his own dislike for the man and how easy it would be to throw an egg at him. It wasn't until Brady heard his father asking about the printed cards that he understood the danger they were in.

"Did you leave any of your cards in Manna when you came through?" Mr. Minton asked.

"Wherever there are people I leave my card," Mr.

172

Lowe said pompously. "I scatter them by the wayside. The sower soweth the word."

Mrs. Minton had stood with a spoon poised in mid-air waiting for the answer. When it came, she began rushing around the kitchen as though a dog were snapping at her heels. She flew in and out of the pantry, over to the breadbox, to the china closet and stove. Mr. Minton took Moses Lowe outside to the pump to wash up.

"I wouldn't give that man a bite of food," Mrs. Minton muttered to Brady, "except that I want him to leave in a hurry. You can't turn a man like that down or cross him, either. He'd be mean enough to stay and argue all night. Quoting the Scripture and trying to convert you to his wicked views." Mrs. Minton slapped some potatoes and cold ham onto a plate and pushed it onto the table. She poured a cup of tea. Then she went to the back door and looked down the road. "All this town needs is to have your pa caught entertaining Moses Lowe! They'd say he was consorting with the wildest abolitionist of all and unfit to preach. No telling what would happen." Mrs. Minton turned to Brady. "See if you can't hurry those men up at the pump. See if we can't get him out of here fast."

But there was no hurrying Moses Lowe. He sat directly before the kitchen window in spite of Mrs. Minton's trying to place him elsewhere. And he talked. He was in no rush, he said, bobbing up and down over his food, picking at the potatoes. He liked to travel by moonlight. Some of his best sermons had been worked

173

out at such times. Then he proceeded to recite some of these sermons, half rising from his chair, his voice almost hysterical, especially when he was repeating certain Biblical passages. When he came to the part about turning the waters of Egypt into blood, Brady watched the veins on Moses Lowe's neck grow and grow until they stood out as big as fishing worms.

At every opportunity Mr. Minton, pacing the floor, tried to take Mr. Lowe to task for his radical stand. But Moses Lowe was not a listener; he was a talker. While he talked, Mrs. Minton sat in her rocking chair, her lips pressed so tightly together that there seemed to be no blood left in them, and she rocked. Faster and faster she rocked.

At last Mr. Lowe finished eating and pushed back his chair. But still he didn't get up. He crossed one leg over his knee. The leather on the sole of his shoe, Brady noticed, was so thin you could see spots where newspaper had been stuffed behind the holes.

"I'm going to travel all through the South on this trip," Mr. Lowe cried. "Through the heart of Egypt land and attack the devil on his own ground."

At that moment an egg spattered against the kitchen window. It ran dripping down the glass and was followed immediately by four other eggs.

Then everything happened at once. Mr. Lowe began shouting. Brady and his father ran out the door, but when Moses Lowe started to follow, he found his way barred. Mrs. Minton was standing with her arms across the doorway.

"I don't care what happens to you, Moses Lowe," she said fiercely. "I'd as soon throw an egg at you myself. But you're not going outside and say things to cause more trouble and get Mr. Minton into a bigger fight. You're going when I tell you to go."

But as it happened, there was no opportunity for a fight. No one was around. The moon was under cover and the dark hillside was giving away no secrets. Although Brady and his father went down the road and beat into the bushes, they could find no one.

When they came back to the house, Moses Lowe had gone and Mrs. Minton was outside, scrubbing furiously at the egg on the kitchen window. On the back steps there was a rock. When Brady went to kick it aside, he saw a note. He and his father took it into the kitchen to read.

WE GIVE MOSES LOWE 15 MINUTES TO GIT OUT. WE GIVE THAT OTHER SLAVE LOVER, THADDEUS MINTON, 48 HOURS. EITHER THAT OR RESIGN FROM THE CHURCH. ELSE WE'LL MAKE IT HOT.

Brady felt his knees suddenly turning watery and queer. He sat down on a chair at the kitchen table. In front of him was Moses Lowe's empty plate and the printed cards scattered and falling onto the floor.

"They're out to get you, Pa," Brady whispered. "What are you going to do?" He had a sudden vision of his father, unable to keep a pulpit, turned into a traveling preacher like Moses Lowe, walking from town to town, his shoe leather thin.

Mr. Minton crumpled the note in his hand, then pushed it into his trousers pocket. "Let's take another turn outside," he said.

This time Mr. Minton and Brady went from one out-building to another, thinking the culprit, whoever he was, might yet be hiding. As they walked together, whispering — Brady and his father — from the barn to the buggy shed, to the chicken house, to the wood-shed, Brady thought how different danger seemed when his father was along. The two figures slipped through the night as one shadow, moving as if they knew each other's minds, as if they shared the same secrets.

Mr. Minton closed the door of the woodshed. "He's not there," he said. "Guess he's got away by now."

"You think he'll come back again tonight?"

"No, I don't."

Brady and his father started up the hill, their feet moving, step by step, in perfect time. This was what it was like to work with his father, Brady thought. This was the way it would be if he could be in on the secret, helping his father, instead of forever on the sidelines, watching and guessing. If only his father would take him all the way into his confidence now, even the note wouldn't seem as frightening. "Forty-eight hours," the note had said. "Else we'll make it hot."

Moss was due to leave for the North in forty-eight hours. Had his father thought about that? Brady won-dered. Had his father figured that if the threat was car-ried out, whatever it was, all the plans for Moss might be upset? Worse yet, the secret itself might be exposed.

The moon came out as Brady and his father stopped at the pump to wash up for the night. They both rolled up their shirt sleeves.

"Forty-eight hours," Brady said. "That's when you'll be going for Mary Dorcas, isn't it?"

"Yes." Mr. Minton pushed the pump handle and water poured down over his arms and Brady's arms, held out together in the moonlight.

Surely now, Brady thought, his father would say that he, too, was worried about the note and needed help. Then maybe, because the situation was so critical, Mr. Minton would tell Brady the secret of the Underground Railroad.

Mr. Minton reached for the towel that hung on the pump handle. "I've been thinking, Brady," he said at last, "that you might like a little holiday. Harvest will be here before you know it; we have a stretch of hard work staring us in the face." He tossed the towel back on the handle and rolled down his sleeves. "I think it would be a good idea for you to go to Washington day after tomorrow and visit Matt overnight. You can leave at noon and come back the following morning." Mr. Minton smiled and gave Brady a quick pat on the shoulder and went into the house.

Brady stood for a long moment, unmoving; then he grabbed the pump handle. He pushed the handle up and down so hard that water splashed on his feet and over his clothes. Oh, he knew well enough why his father was suggesting the trip. Any other time it would have been different, but now! Brady held one hand under the pump and soused cold water up to his face. Suggesting the trip didn't mean that his father trusted him; as a matter of fact, it meant just the opposite. This was his father's way of getting rid of him. Just when the danger would be at its greatest, when Moss was due to leave, when the note writer had promised to make it "hot" — that was when his father wanted him out of the way. As far as his father was concerned, Brady thought, he was a hindrance rather than a help. He jerked the pump handle again and this time he put his head under the pump and let the water pour over his hair and run stinging down his neck.

Chapter Fifteen

As far back as Brady could remember, he'd pictured what a great day it would be when he saddled up one of his father's horses and rode off to Washington alone. He'd feel as if he owned the world — swinging over the countryside, stopping to pass the time of day with folks he didn't know — strangers traveling a distance just as he was.

But the way the trip had finally come about, Brady would rather do anything than go to Washington. He'd rather stay home and clean the chicken house. Or go to bed with a case of measles. There was no pride in going to Washington the way Brady was going. Even when he'd started on the trip and ridden past a group of school friends in Manna, Brady couldn't find any pleasure in calling out the news that he was off to Washington alone. Even when he saw Laban Williams in the group and saw Laban's mouth drop open in surprise, Brady couldn't work up any enthusiasm. A week or so ago it would have been different. There was nothing Brady would have enjoyed more than lording it over Laban Williams who, Brady knew, still hadn't made his first trip alone.

But today the sight of Laban Williams was almost more than Brady could bear.

"You stayin' overnight?" Laban asked and there was a look of cunning in his eyes.

"None of your business."

Brady spurred his horse and galloped furiously out of town, trying to ride away from all the pictures that Laban Williams brought to mind. The drawing of the man in tar and feathers, for instance. Drover Hull's deserted cabin with possibly a corpse in it. Raw eggs splashing across a window. And Laban's eyes when he'd asked Brady if he was staying overnight. There was a reason behind that question, sure as shooting. Perhaps a plot.

Brady urged his horse faster over the stretch of

straight road outside Manna, but there was no riding away from his fears. At any pace Brady tried, the horse's hoofbeats tapped out the words foremost in Brady's mind. "*Forty-eight hours, forty-eight hours,*" the hoofbeats said. "*Forty-eight, forty-eight . . .*" all the long way into Washington. Up Chestnut Street, down Main Street, past the town square and courthouse. Brady looked up at the round globe on top of the courthouse where the weather-vane arrow, slowly shifting direction, veered north. Cold tonight, Brady thought, and he turned down Beau Street.

Mrs. Paul's boardinghouse, where Matt had been living since he became a professor, was across the street from the college. Brady found it easily, and as he rang the bell he told himself that once he was inside, he'd feel more natural. He'd forget everything else and start enjoying the holiday.

But when Brady stepped inside, he was struck immediately by what a strange place this boardinghouse was. It was like a museum or an ancient tomb of some sort filled with queer objects meant for a life quite different from anything that Brady had ever known. On one side of the dark entrance hall there was a stand supporting a small brass Chinese pagoda. Inside the pagoda a lighted candle flung long, eerie shadows across the floor and up the staircase. The walls on all sides were covered with scrolls, plates, odd utensils and weapons, all of which, Mrs. Paul explained, had been collected by her father, a professor who had traveled four times around the world. Mrs. Paul, who was something of a curiosity herself, waved Brady upstairs and told him Matt was in the first room to the right, just behind the statue of the Buddha. You couldn't miss it, she said, and that was true enough. The statue almost blocked the way to Matt's door — a knee-high figure of a seated fat man, bare to the waist and grinning, for petey's sakes.

Even when Matt opened the door and shouted, "Hey Snapper, where'd you come from?", Brady couldn't shake off the strangeness of the house. He hadn't felt like himself when he'd started on this trip; he didn't feel any more so now.

"How did you get here?" Matt grinned. "You must have been a model of good behavior to get off the farm before the summer was over."

"Um." Brady grunted uncomfortably and sat down on the corner of the bed. It was queer how, after coming so far, there didn't seem much to say.

"Well, what's new, boy?" Matt asked.

"Nothing much." There was a pile of examination papers on Matt's desk that he must have been correcting. On the bed there were more papers, books, and newspapers. Brady picked up one of the books; he couldn't even understand its title.

"Oh, come on now," Matt laughed, pushing aside enough papers so he could sit down on his desk. "There must be some news."

Brady shrugged. "Guess you heard from Uncle Earl about the church splitting over Pa's sermon."

Matt nodded. "How did it go last Sunday?"

"There was no trouble. Only empty pews."

"Anything else happen?"

Brady twisted his hands together. If he could only tell the whole story! A person as smart as Matt could set you straight in your thinking. "Well, Moses Lowe invited himself to our house the other night." At least that much was not a secret.

Matt whistled.

"Someone threw eggs at the kitchen window while Moses Lowe was there. We didn't find out who did it."

Matt got up and walked to the window. "I wonder how long Pa can hold to his moderate position. In times like these, it isn't easy."

"Well, I hope he doesn't turn into an abolitionist," Brady said quickly. "I've never seen one yet that wasn't at least part-way wild in the head." Brady sighed. Here he was on a holiday and the first thing he did was get into a discussion on slavery. He picked up a newspaper lying on the bed and looked at the masthead. The paper was published in Boston. *The Liberator*, it was called. Brady had heard of *The Liberator*, all right; everyone had. It was the paper put out by William Lloyd Garrison, the leader and founder of the abolitionist movement.

Brady pointed to the paper. "You haven't turned out to be an abolitionist, for petey's sakes, have you, Matt?"

"Do you think I'm wild in the head?" Matt smiled, but he didn't exactly answer the question outright, Brady noticed.

"You wouldn't call a gentleman like John Quincy Adams wild in the head either, would you?" Matt went on.

Brady admitted that he wouldn't.

"Well, you know what John Quincy Adams said? In January of this year he was talking to the House of Representatives about the end of slavery. 'Whether peaceably or by blood, it shall be accomplished. By whatever way, I say let it come.' That's what he said."

"Is that the way you feel?"

Matt nodded. "It's the way I'm beginning to feel. The country can't go on torn and divided and full of hatred the way it is. I'd like to see the issue settled once and for all."

"But the abolitionists are the ones that have caused so much of the hatred," Brady objected.

"Some of them. That's true. But we've all gone too far and said too much to hope for a compromise. And Brady —" Matt hesitated. "Don't judge all abolitionists by Moses Lowe. Or by Mr. McKain either."

Now Brady really was mixed up. It was one thing to get used to your brother being a professor; it was another thing to get used to his being an abolitionist.

But Matt was laughing. "Don't look so distressed, Snapper," he said. "Being an abolitionist isn't the worst thing in the world. I bet you two cents before this thing is settled, Pa will be one too. Now let's go upstreet and have a glass of ice cream. We'll forget all about politics and slavery while we celebrate your holiday."

Matt went out of his way to give Brady a good time, taking him on a regular sightseeing tour, introducing him to other professors and friends. By all rights Brady should have forgotten his worries. He might have, too, if he and Matt had gone into the confectioner's store just five minutes earlier. As it was, they were standing outside, talking to a group of Matt's friends, when three men came out of the Washington Hall Tavern next door. At first Brady scarcely noticed the men, but their talk, as they stood a few yards away, became more and more raucous. One voice in particular was louder than the others and somehow faintly familiar. Brady looked over and there was the slave catcher that Brady and Range had trailed earlier in the summer. The slave catcher's head was thrown back in a great rumbling laugh. The jagged red scar on his cheek danced every which way.

Almost at the same moment the slave catcher caught sight of Brady. "Where are your crutches, boy?" he called loudly and then, letting loose another roll of laughter, he drifted down the street with his friends.

Brady's face turned a flaming red.

"You know that man?" Matt asked curiously.

Brady nodded. "Range and I saw him once in Manna. I was fooling around with Tar Adams' crutches at the time."

"You should have hit him over the head with the crutches. He's one of the most successful slave catchers around."

"He has some partners with him this time," one of Matt's friends observed. "They're making the Washington Hall their headquarters."

"There are a lot of them around. One or two of the Southern states have just raised the bounty on slaves, I hear." This was another of Matt's friends talking.

"Slave catchers are combing the county. Tearing down haystacks to look inside."

Brady felt his insides turning as cold as if he'd swallowed a chunk of ice. He went through the motions of enjoying the rest of the day because he didn't know what else to do, but when night came there was no pretense left in him. He lay in the big four-poster bed beside Matt and gave himself over to his fears. "Tearing down haystacks," Matt's friend had said. "Combing the country." Brady lay still as a stone, picturing a whole bevy of slave catchers converging on Moss while Bill and Laban Williams stood there grinning like that crazy statue of the Buddha. And then outside on Beau Street a horse galloped past. *"Forty-eight hours,"* the hoofbeats said. *"Forty-eight . . . forty-eight . . ."*

Suddenly Brady knew what he had to do. He crept out of bed quietly so he wouldn't disturb Matt's sleep. He dressed, found a pencil and paper and wrote Matt a note. He supposed no matter what he said in the note, Matt would think Brady had been homesick. Well, let Matt think Brady was a baby. Let Matt think anything at all. Brady had to go home.

Chapter Sixteen

As soon as Brady saw the Minton house sitting on top of the hill just where it belonged and the barn and the Sermon House, the buggy shed, and the woodshed, all lighted up by the moon, he felt a surge of relief. Even the back door was locked which meant his parents were upstairs, asleep. At least his mother was probably asleep. His father might be lying awake, lis-

187

tening, unwilling to alarm his wife. In any case, Brady moved as quietly as possible so no one would know he was home. He was going to stay outside all night. On guard. Sitting by the Sermon House, hiding in the shadow of the barn, crouching by the back doorsteps — his eyes searching, his ears tensed for every sound.

But first he had to put Jenny, his horse, away. In order to make the least noise, he led her over the grass instead of riding her up the dirt driveway as he normally would. It was strange how Jenny seemed almost to sense the need for quiet too. She put her feet down so nicely and made no attempt to make that last-minute dash into the barn which she sometimes took a notion to do. In fact she co-operated so well, it was a surprise when after her saddle had been removed, she suddenly for no reason at all began acting skittish. She tossed her head up and down and shied when Brady went to un-bridle her.

"For petey's sakes, Jenny, hold still," Brady growled. "It's hard enough to do this with no more light than that little bit of moonlight coming in the door."

But Jenny's nervousness was contagious. In a minute the other two horses, Beauty and Buck, were moving restlessly in their stalls. Beauty, the black mare, suddenly raised up on her hind legs and pawed the air. Brady wondered if maybe his own fears were setting the horses off.

"Whoa there, Jenny, whoa. What's got into you?"

Sometimes an approaching thunderstorm could upset Jenny but tonight the sky was clear.

Then Brady saw the fire licking at the far end of the barn. Already it was too big to stamp out. His first inclination was to run screaming for help, but when he tried his voice, it wasn't there. He thought about rushing outside to see how the fire had started, but before he could get his legs moving he remembered what a person was supposed to do when a barn caught fire. The first thing was to get the horses out quietly before they became too frightened to move.

"Whoa there, Beauty. Hold on." Brady's voice cracked but at least it was working. "I'll be back for you in a minute."

Even as he was talking, he was leading Jenny out of the barn. He tied her quickly to the nearest tree and ran back for the other two horses. Grabbing a couple of ropes, Brady slipped one around Beauty's neck and the other around Buck's. He had no trouble leading Buck out, but when he came back for Beauty, she was more alarmed than ever. The fire hadn't taken over yet but it was gaining. The noise was like a giant rat gnawing in the corner. Beauty pulled against the rope, rolled her eyes, and neighed wildly.

"Come on, girl. Steady now." Brady's mouth was dry.

"Come on." He tried again desperately, using every trick he'd ever known to make a horse mind. Then like a lesson he'd forgotten, it came to Brady what he had to do next. He reached for a saddle blanket hanging on Beauty's stall and threw it over her head as a blindfold.

And it worked. Beauty followed Brady out of the barn.

Thank goodness, Brady whispered, thank goodness. Thank goodness he'd been home. Thank goodness it was summer and the cows were in the pasture and not in the barn. He tied Beauty up, leaving the saddle blanket over her head.

As soon as she was secure, Brady opened his mouth and shouted. "Pa! Pa!" Every bit of strength he possessed went into that shout and into his legs as he raced toward the back door. As intent as he was, however, out of the corner of his eye he saw something move behind the barn. It was a person trampling through the vegetable garden. Running. A person about the size of Laban Williams. But Brady couldn't go after him. Not now. The barn came first. "Pa! Pa!" Brady shouted again.

Mr. Minton was already outside, pulling his overalls on over his nightshirt as he ran to the pump. Mrs. Minton was behind him. In a moment the three of them had formed a bucket line. Brady's place was at the pump, working for all he was worth. As soon as one or two buckets were filled, Mrs. Minton took them to her husband and returned to Brady whatever buckets were empty. Mr. Minton, too, rushed back and forth with water but as soon as he threw one bucketful on the fire, it seemed, a flame would shoot up in a different spot. There was no getting ahead of it. As fast and as furiously as they worked, the flame spread until all at once half the roof was on fire.

"It's reached the hayloft," Mr. Minton said, looking down at the useless bucket of water still in his hand. "It's reached the hayloft." And in a sudden burst of fury, Mr. Minton threw bucket and all into the fire.

For a moment the three Mintons stood helplessly, watching their barn burn. Then as if he were coming out of a daze, Mr. Minton ran for the barn door. "Come on, Brady, let's save the saddles," he called over his shoulder.

The saddles hung on pegs just inside the barn door. It seemed safe enough to make one quick trip inside the door and out again. Brady gathered up an armload and dumped it on the ground. Mr. Minton, too, gathered what he could, but on the way out, he tripped over a rein that dangled from his arm. He was thrown to the floor of the barn and the wind was knocked out of him. Before he could get to his feet, there was a cracking over his head and a portion of a beam from the burning roof fell onto his right leg.

Later Brady could never remember the sequence of what followed. He felt as if he were part of a slow-motion nightmare, working with his mother, both of them unbearably clumsy. Although it seemed like an eternity, actually it wasn't long until they had freed Mr. Minton's leg and pulled him to safety. Sometime in the middle of the nightmare Range and his father had rushed up the hill and they had helped. Some friends from as far as Manna, attracted by the flames, were there too. The sky above the Minton hill was sunset color.

As soon as other people came, Brady found himself on the sidelines again. Dr. Scott and Mr. Fergus, both among the first to arrive, carried Mr. Minton upstairs to his room. The inside of the house, which normally at this time of night was ruled by Mr. Potter's clock, was turned in a matter of moments, it seemed, into a hive of activity. When Brady tried to find out about his father, he was answered by a lot of different people in half sentences. "Don't know yet. Maybe a broken leg. Unconscious part of the time."

Brady went outside. The driveway was filled with people watching the barn burn. Everything was being done that needed to be done. Brady walked around to the other side of the barn, alone. Somehow he didn't want to stand among a lot of folks saying wasn't that a sight and wasn't that a shame.

He took his place at the far end of the vegetable patch where the heat was so strong it hurt, but he didn't move. He just stood there and watched the barn roof cave in and one by one the walls fall and gradually the fire, that had been a roaring mountain, ebb until its size was more believable. Brady could look at the fire now and at the same time he could begin to think.

What was going to happen to Moss? The agent was likely waiting now at Uncle Will's and how in thunder was Moss going to get there? Brady's father certainly couldn't take Moss anywhere. Brady began pacing back and forth, keeping one eye on the fire that had reduced the barn to nothing but a huge pile of burning trash. As the heat lessened, he walked into the vegetable garden. Some of the vegetables were scorched and the whole crop of peas was gone. And in the light of the fire Brady could see where the patch had been trampled.

By Laban Williams. Brady doubled up his fists. He was sure Laban Williams had been the one. There were some fresh footprints. Brady put his own foot down next to them. They were about the same size. The other person's footprints, however, were running footprints; the mark of the toes dug deep into the ground. Then Brady saw something else. Lying on the ground was Laban Williams' treasured pocket knife. Brady picked it up. There was no mistaking it with the big W carved on it. He'd seen it too many times and heard too many stories about it not to recognize it. Everyone else had heard those stories too. Brady dropped the knife into his pocket. If his father and his Uncle Earl wanted evidence that Laban Williams had been here tonight when the fire started, here was the evidence. *"We'll make it hot."* That's what the note had said. Well, once his Uncle Earl had hold of this knife, he could make it hot for Bill and Laban Williams too. And the sooner, the better.

Brady ran back to the house. A plan was beginning to form in his mind, but he had to see his father. It might be a good plan and then again it might not. In any case, there was no time to lose.

Most of the people had left, now that the fire had all but spent itself. Dr. Scott, however, was still inside, and as Brady reached the back steps, he met Mr. Fergus coming out the door.

"I'm going home to get my wife," Mr. Fergus said. "I think she'd be a help and a comfort to your mother tonight. She needs another woman here."

"How's Pa?"

"He's in a great deal of pain, Brady. He has some burns and a badly broken leg. Dr. Scott is about to set the leg."

"I've got to see Pa."

Brady started on but Mr. Fergus put a hand on Brady's arm.

"How did the fire start, son?"

Brady tightened his mouth. "It was set."

"Any idea who did it?"

Instead of answering, Brady reached into his pocket for Laban Williams' knife. He held it out on the palm of his hand. Everyone knew that knife.

Again when Brady started to go, Mr. Fergus detained him. "I never thought Bill Williams would go that far." Mr. Fergus spoke haltingly and studied the smoldering fire, his eyes troubled. "There's more behind this than the issue of slavery. I don't like it." At last he took his hand away from Brady's arm. "Tell your pa I'll be in church the next time he preaches."

Brady didn't stop to digest Mr. Fergus' news. Already he was bounding up the steps. But when he reached his father's room, the door was closed.

Mrs. Minton came out.

"I have to see Pa," Brady said.

Mrs. Minton shook her head. "Not tonight, Brady. He's in no condition to talk to anyone." She went to the linen closet for a sheet to tear into strips of bandage.

"I have to see Pa. Just for a minute. Alone," Brady insisted.

"Absolutely no." Mrs. Minton stopped to put her

arm briefly around Brady's shoulder. "Dr. Scott is about to set his leg. It will be a long operation. The best thing you can do is stay out of the way."

Brady stared at the bedroom door as it closed in his face. He'd have to make the decision alone. Right or wrong, he'd have to decide for himself. If he stayed home and did nothing, his father would never discover that Brady knew about the Underground Railroad. Even with a broken leg, his father would likely find some way of taking care of Moss and getting him to Canada another time. Staying home would certainly be the safe thing for Brady to do.

Slowly he went down the stairs, his hand sliding over the banister. At the bottom step Mr. Parley Potter's clock struck — once, twice. If Brady left now, he'd reach Uncle Will's by breakfast time.

He wrote a note and left it on the kitchen table. *I have gone for Mary Dorcas*, he wrote. *When I go through Washington, I'll tell Uncle Earl about the fire and about Pa.*

He guessed he'd see Uncle Earl and give him the knife on the way back, after he'd delivered Moss safely to the agent. Brady closed his eyes. Oh, he hoped he'd get Moss there safely. He hoped he was doing the right thing.

Chapter Seventeen

WHEN BRADY went into the buggy shed, he found the road wagon packed and ready to go. Barrels of clothes for the school in Canada were lashed to three sides of the wagon. The fourth side and the center of the wagon were piled high with blankets and loose clothes. It was under this loose pile that Mr. Minton had evidently planned to hide Moss.

Brady ran to the Sermon House. Before he had finished tapping, Moss had answered and a second later the door was open. At other times Brady had seen Moss frightened momentarily by one thing or another, but now Moss stood inside the door almost overcome, it seemed, by his fear. His voice was shaking and his eyes held the same look of terror that Beauty's had had in the barn. For a minute Brady was afraid maybe Moss was too frightened to co-operate, but as soon as Moss understood what had happened and what the plans were, he brought himself quickly under control. He went into the Jerusalem room for Lisha and at the open door of the Sermon House, he set the mouse free. Both boys watched as Lisha hesitated a moment, then disappeared among the weeds.

"You ready?" Brady whispered.

Moss nodded. "Just one thing I got to know first, Master Brady." He stepped back from the door where the light from the barn couldn't reach him. "You're sure you want to do this? You thought twice about it?"

"I'm sure."

"You can get into a peck of trouble. Even if things go just right, your pa may not take kindly to what you're doin'. You thought of that?"

"I've thought of it."

"A person like me ain't worth that big a risk, Master Brady. You change your mind now and I won't feel bad."

"I've made up my mind."

It was strange, Brady thought as he and Moss made

their way stealthily to the buggy shed, how sure he did feel about what he was doing. Scared, yes, plenty scared, but still sure he wanted to do it. He went about the business of hiding Moss under the clothes as though he'd been planning it for days. Then he went down to the pasture where the horses had been put during the fire. Buck was the first to come when Brady whistled, so it was Buck a few minutes later who pulled Brady and Moss and the road wagon down the driveway.

As he drove out, Brady looked up at his father's window. Every candle in the house must be burning in that room to give Dr. Scott the light he needed. Brady pressed his lips together at the thought of what was going on up there; then he slapped the reins down on Buck's back.

There was no way, however, that a person could hurry a road wagon. As many times as Brady had ridden in one, he had never been as aware of what a cumbersome, poky, exasperating thing a road wagon was. He pulled down on his head an old hat of his father's that he'd picked up at the last minute in the buggy shed. He hunched over in the wagon seat. If there were any slave catchers around, maybe they'd mistake him for a teamster with a load of dry goods. It was a cinch that in this jiggly old wagon Brady Minton couldn't outrun anyone.

But the first person Brady saw on the road, he didn't want to run from. As he rounded a corner on the way to Manna, he suddenly came upon Laban Williams, ambling along as though it were his custom to be out

on the road at two or three o'clock in the morning.
Laban looked over his shoulder as he heard the wagon
approach, but he didn't recognize Brady.

Laban must have been hiding out somewhere, Brady
thought, making sure the barn burned all the way to the
ground.

Brady slipped out of the wagon seat and led Buck up
the hill. Brady could feel the knife in his pocket, a hard
spot on his leg as he walked, and this was a comfort.
But as he watched Laban a few steps ahead, moving
slowly, tuckered out from the night's work, all at once
the knife wasn't enough. Oh, the knife would likely
bring Bill and Laban Williams to court but that might
take a while. And this was tonight. Brady could smell
the smoke from the barn. Even on this hill he could
smell it. And the sky was still red.

"Hey, Laban!"

At the sound of Brady's voice, Laban jumped. He
turned around and when he saw it was Brady Minton
leading a horse and wagon, Laban's eyes squinted, narrow as a cat's.

He's gathering up his wits, Brady thought. He thinks
I don't know.

"Where are *you* goin', Brady Minton?" Laban asked.

"I was going to ask you the same question."

"I'm goin' home, but you're not. You're goin' the
opposite way. With a wagonload of household goods,
looks like. You folks movin' now that your barn's
burned?"

"No, we've no notion of moving." Brady brought the horse and wagon to a standstill beside Laban. "You've been to the fire, I suppose."

"Yea. I was there. Like everyone else, I seen the sky and I went for a look." But as though he sensed something wrong, Laban began to back away. "What's wrong with that?" he whined. "Half the town was lookin'."

"I'll tell you what was wrong with it," Brady said fiercely. "You were the first one there. You set the fire." He grabbed Laban by the collar. "And I've got your knife right here in my pocket to prove it. You dropped it behind the barn when you ran away. Now I'm taking it to my Uncle Earl in Washington and he'll show it to the judge. What do you think of that?"

All at once then Brady had had enough of talking. He doubled up his fist and punched Laban Williams in the face as hard as he could punch. Laban went sprawling on the side of the road, and when he went to get up, Brady knocked him down again. He was still on his back when Brady drove off.

For a short while after this encounter with Laban Williams, the trip to Uncle Will's didn't seem quite so dangerous. Brady could still feel Laban's face against his hand. A good solid smack. If anything did develop on the trip, he thought, he might just be able to handle it.

But it was a long way from Manna to Uncle Will's, and the confidence that Brady had felt after punching Laban turned out to be only a little spurt of confidence, after all. Long before he even reached Washington, Brady felt his courage slipping. It was one thing to take care of a boy like Laban, the same size as Brady and at heart something of a coward; it would be another thing to deal with a group of slave catchers or, for that matter, even one slave catcher who decided that the cargo Brady Minton was hauling looked suspicious.

Brady passed a field of haystacks and was reminded of what Matt's friend had said. Suddenly an owl's hoot sounded in the distance; it was like a warning. Brady shivered and reached back into the wagon for something to put around his shoulders. In the pile of clothes he found an old coat and put it on.

As the minutes dragged by, the slow, plodding, turtle pace of the road wagon became all but unendurable. It seemed to Brady that he was at a standstill, like a target, while around him the whole countryside was alive and moving with mischief. Shadows leaped out from graveyards; trees shook suddenly and mysteriously as if moved by the hand of a hidden enemy. A fox darted across the path of the wagon, its eyes gleaming in the moonlight. Even the clouds looked ominous. Brady tried to find the North Star, but it was lost. What he saw instead was a faint glow in the east. Not exactly a glow, either, but a place in the sky where the night had worn thin. By the time he reached Washington, it would be daylight. His shoulders and back ached as if he were pulling the road wagon instead of Buck. If there was one thing Brady had wanted, it was to go through Washington under cover of darkness.

But when he started up Main Street, the sky was the color of an eggshell, the way it is the first thing in the morning. Cocks were crowing, a few cats were stirring on doorsteps, but otherwise the town was asleep. Hunched over his knees, his hat pulled down as far as it would go, Brady thought he'd never heard such a racket as the wagon made on the quiet street. Creaking and groaning loud enough to wake up the whole town, for petey's sakes, and every slave catcher in it. But it was in front of the Washington Hall Tavern that the wagon made the most noise. As they went over a deeply rutted spot, the barrels rattled against each other like drums beating. Buck let out a loud series of disgusted snorts. Brady didn't dare look to the right or the left. A door slammed some place behind him; a window was thrown open. Maybe someone had come out of the tavern. Maybe right now someone was following the wagon, sizing up its load, waiting for an appropriate time and a lonely place to spring at it.

Brady didn't look around until he was all the way out of Washington and in the country again. Then he turned his head. No one was there. At least no one that Brady could see. But the road from here to Uncle Will's ran through an uncleared area. There was a heavy growth of trees on both sides — giant-size trees that had likely been here before any white man had heard of America. The trees bent over the road and all but shut out the daylight. A slave catcher could sneak along close to the road and a person wouldn't even see him.

Brady didn't rest easy until he saw the covered bridge

ahead. The other side of the bridge was farm country and on a clear day you could see Uncle Will's place from there. Even as a little boy Brady had breathed easier when he'd seen the bridge. These particular woods, the way they pressed so close to the road and hung over it, did sometimes give a person a spooky feeling and that was a fact.

As Brady approached the bridge, he felt distinctly better. If anyone was going to challenge him, he would have done it by now. Brady decided to stop the wagon for a minute and slip out back and say good-by to Moss. There might not be a chance when they got to Uncle Will's.

Brady pulled over to the side of the road, but when he went to get down from the wagon, he found his arms and legs cramped from the long ride. It seemed strange to be in a world that wasn't jogging up and down, rattling and creaking. For the first time in hours Brady could hear something besides the wagon wheels. Although he couldn't see it, he could hear the river rushing under the bridge. He pictured the way it broke into the trees and the secret, rocky caves along the banks that he'd explored once or twice when he'd been at Uncle Will's for a visit.

At the back of the wagon, Brady lifted up the blankets. Moss was lying on his stomach, his head cradled in his arms. He jerked up his head.

"We're about there," Brady said. "How did you make out?"

"About shook to pieces." Moss grinned. "Reckon

that lake won't shake me any more than this wagon did."

"Did you think we'd never make it?"

"No. I figured you'd do it." Moss' eyes as he looked at Brady were full of admiration. "I'm glad you stopped. I got something to tell you."

Brady leaned up against the wagon. He'd been sitting tense in one position for so long that he was trembling all over.

"I got me my second name. Don't know why I didn't think of it before," he said. "I'm real proud of it." He hesitated. "Moss Brady. From now on, that's my name. Moss Brady."

Brady swallowed, unable for a moment to find his voice. "I'm proud too," he said finally. Then all at once he wished he had something to give Moss. Something permanent. He reached into his pocket, but of course it was a futile gesture. He wasn't going to find a silver shilling or any other ready-made gift in his pocket. There was only a penny, one that Uncle Earl had given him weeks before. As Brady fingered the coin, he suddenly remembered what Mr. Parley Potter had said. If you hang onto your first piece of money, it will bring you luck all your life. He hadn't said a word about its having to be a silver shilling.

"Have you ever had any money of your own?" Brady asked abruptly.

"No."

"Not even a penny?"

"Nothin'."

Brady took the penny from his pocket and pressed

it into Moss' hand. "Don't spend it. Hang onto it and it will bring you luck all your life."

Moss opened his mouth to thank Brady but at that moment there was a rustling behind Brady and a footstep on the road.

"Who are you and where you goin'?" a hoarse voice called.

Brady dropped the blanket over Moss and swung around. When he saw who was there, his heart jumped to his throat. It was like seeing a ghost. Indeed, maybe he was seeing a ghost.

Drover Hull stood on the road, his white hair blowing and a knotted walking stick in his hand.

"You heard me," Drover Hull repeated. "I asked your name." He spit in the road, moved closer to Brady and peered under his hat.

"Ain't you Reverend Minton's son?"

Brady nodded, pressing his teeth together to keep them from chattering.

"Where's your pa at?"

Brady's back was against the wagon and his hands clung to the side of it. "Pa's home," he whispered. "He has a broken leg."

Drover Hull began walking around the wagon, looking at it from all sides and roaring as he went. "Why in the blue blazes did he send a boy like you? Why didn't he send someone like Tar Adams that we could trust?" He jerked his thumb toward the spot where Moss was hiding. "I could have taken that boy north another time. Why didn't he wait?" Drover shook his stick at

Brady. "You chased me away from my cabin, poking around where you weren't wanted. Am I goin' to have to give up my cave here because of you?" He pointed toward the river, his eyes burning and his mouth all but frothing with anger. He was like a prophet or a sorcerer of some kind who at any minute might crash down his stick and change everything he saw into something else.

But instead of a sorcerer, Drover Hull was obviously the agent who was to take Moss to Canada. From what he said, Drover must have been working with Mr. Minton right from the start, but Brady was too frightened to pursue that thought any further now. He was too frightened even to admit that coming here had been his own idea, not his father's.

Drover Hull went right on talking. "Why didn't you stop on the other side of the bridge like your pa and I planned it? Suppose you thought you knew better, huh?" Drover flipped back the blanket that was covering Moss and at the sight of the runaway boy, his voice gentled somewhat. "Come on out, boy," Drover said. "You're goin' to be all right. You ain't to blame for this mix-up."

Brady stood aside as Moss backed slowly out of the wagon, not too eager, it appeared, to make Drover Hull's acquaintance. But as soon as his feet were on the ground, Moss turned to Drover and spoke up as if Drover Hull were just any man, for petey's sakes, instead of a combination hermit, ghost, scarecrow, and heaven knows what else.

"You can trust this boy, mister," Moss said. "You don't need to worry none about him."

Hearing Moss gave Brady the courage to speak too.

"I'm not going to tell any secrets, Mr. Hull," Brady said pleadingly.

For a moment Drover Hull stared at the two boys so intensely that his eyes seemed to be burning a hole all the way inside them.

"I can't see how a boy could change much in a few months. And your pa didn't trust you then, Brady Minton," he said. "Don't know if it's safe to go on with the station or not." Drover Hull spit again, hitting the hub of the wagon wheel this time dead center. "Well, maybe your pa knows what he's doin'," he grumbled. "As long as he sent you."

Brady stood by the wagon, the world spinning around him and the trees closing in. All he could do was whisper a good-by when Drover led Moss away. He, Brady Minton, had been the cause of Drover's closing his cabin and moving away. Brady remembered the morning his father had come back from the fields, covered with broomstraw. Likely he'd just returned from telling Drover Hull they'd have to find another hideout because Brady had discovered this one. And how would his father feel now? Just the same as Drover Hull, most likely. Like Drover, his father wouldn't believe a boy could change in a couple of months. His father might even feel obliged to give up the Underground station altogether. In any case, his father would lose his Canadian agent if Drover Hull heard that Brady had come on his own today.

Brady watched Drover and Moss make their way toward the riverbank. Just before they disappeared from sight, Drover turned around. "You take that load along to your Uncle Will's now. He'll know what to do with it. I don't take it this trip."

As Brady climbed into the wagon, he felt strangely lightheaded. He couldn't remember when he'd last slept or eaten. When he tried to think about home, his mind whirled. It was all he could do to sit up and hold onto the reins until he got to Uncle Will's.

Chapter Eighteen

A T FIRST Brady was too tired to know what was going on about him at Uncle Will's. He couldn't
have told what he had to eat or what questions the folks
asked him or what he answered. Of course, he had told
them right away about the fire and his father's accident.
And he did remember having something to eat and his
grandmother's insisting that he go to bed for a couple

of hours. He felt better after that. In a private conversation in the bedroom, he told Uncle Will about the trip with Moss and about Laban and Bill Williams; in turn Brady found out a few things about the Underground station. It appeared that Parley Potter, Tar Adams, Drover Hull and the two Minton men had been operating the station for some time. Drover Hull was a mighty peculiar man, Uncle Will said, and could be as ornery as all get out, but he was a good agent. He had such a high opinion of freedom, he'd been a hermit rather than be beholden to anybody. And he'd turn himself inside out to help a runaway. Tar Adams wasn't a cripple at all, Uncle Will said; he just pretended to be because he was safer that way.

But in all this talk Brady never admitted that bringing Moss had been his own idea and not his father's. He didn't mention that he'd simply stumbled on the secret himself, that his father had never confided in him and likely never would. Like Drover Hull, Uncle Will somehow assumed that when Mr. Minton couldn't come, he'd sent Brady in his place. And Brady let him go on thinking that. It was going to be hard enough to face his father without having to face Uncle Will too. As a matter of fact, it was the thought of facing his father that had Brady so distracted. In his mind he was already at home, upstairs in his father's bedroom, waiting to hear what his father said when he heard the full story. Until that moment, nothing that happened to Brady seemed important or even very real.

Uncle Will suggested that rather than make the long

trip in the road wagon, Brady should return on horse-back, alone. He could take one of Uncle Will's horses. As for Mary Dorcas, she and Uncle Will would follow in the road wagon as soon as Buck had had a chance to rest up. The next morning or, perhaps, even sooner. Besides, it was important, Uncle Will said, that Brady get that knife to Uncle Earl as soon as possible.

Brady didn't stop to wonder what his mother would think when he came back without Mary Dorcas. He hardly even noticed Mary Dorcas, prancing around, chattering as usual. And when he took a letter Uncle Will gave him, he stuffed it into his pocket without paying much attention to Uncle Will's instructions that Brady give the letter to his father. All Brady knew was that if he went home by horseback, he'd get there sooner.

Even on horseback, however, the trip seemed long and the road stretched ahead endlessly. Brady lost all sense of time and had no way of measuring it. The sky had turned gray and he couldn't tell where the sun was. But sometime in the late afternoon Brady stopped at the courthouse in Washington to give Uncle Earl the knife. He told his uncle about seeing Laban run through the vegetable patch, about finding the footprints and then the knife. He talked quickly, in a hurry to get through the story, but when he came to the part about punching Laban in the face, he lingered over the telling. That punch was a satisfying thing to recall and that was a fact.

"Did you tell Laban you had his knife?" Uncle Earl asked.

"I sure did. I told him I was bringing it to you."

Uncle Earl grinned and told Brady he had the makings of a fine deputy. It was even possible, Uncle Earl said, that Bill Williams and his family would clear out altogether rather than face the music in court. At least Bill would have to withdraw his name as candidate for sheriff. And he'd have to quit fighting the Mintons.

"I'll tell Matt about the fire and your pa's accident," Uncle Earl wound up. "The two of us will be down tonight sometime, though I don't know what help we can be. Seems to me you're your pa's best helper." He thumped Brady on the shoulder and walked with him to the street where his horse was tied. "Your pa will rest easy with you around to take over," Uncle Earl said.

If Uncle Earl only knew, Brady thought as he rode away.

Brady's trip finally came to an end in the early evening. He ran the horse up the driveway and then pulled to an abrupt halt. He'd been about to go into the barn, but of course the barn wasn't there. There was only a black, charred square on the ground and the prongs of a pitchfork sticking out of the ashes. Mrs. Minton came to the back door; Range was sitting on the doorstep.

Brady slipped off the horse, all at once overcome by how complicated everything was going to be — all the questions his mother would ask, all the explanations that had to be made. He didn't know where to begin.

"How's Pa?" he asked.

"Getting along as well as can be expected. He's asleep now," Mrs. Minton said.

"Can I see him?"

"As soon as he wakes up. I have a bowl of stew in the kitchen for you, Brady. Likely you're hungry."

It was queer, Brady thought as he sat down at the kitchen table, that his mother seemed to have something else on her mind instead of Mary Dorcas. Then a terrible thought struck Brady. Maybe his mother and Range were hiding something. Maybe there was some bad news.

"Pa's all right, isn't he?" Brady whispered. "Nothing went wrong, did it?"

"No. It was just what Dr. Scott said — a leg badly broken in two places. A few burns. He's on the mend but it will take a long time."

Relief flooded through Brady as though it were a medicine. "Uncle Will's bringing Mary Dorcas home the first thing in the morning," he volunteered. "As soon as Buck's rested up. I told Uncle Earl about the fire too. He and Matt will be here tonight."

Mrs. Minton sat down at the table beside Brady. She leaned forward. "Everything went well, did it?" she asked quietly.

Brady stared down at his beef stew. The way his mother spoke, it was almost as if she guessed about Moss, for petey's sakes.

"Why, yes," Brady said, not looking up. "I didn't run into any trouble at all."

As his mother ladled out another spoonful of stew, Brady eyed her thoughtfully. If she was suspicious, there was no way of telling. And there never would be.

"Does Pa know I went?"

"He asked where you were and I told him."

Brady finished his stew. He took a piece of bread and ran it around the edge of the bowl.

"Did you tell him I took the road wagon?"

"He asked me to go into the buggy shed and check and I did."

"What did he say?"

"He wasn't pleased."

At that moment there was a tapping on the floor above.

"Your father's awake," Mrs. Minton said.

Brady pushed his bowl aside. As he stood up, Mrs. Minton smiled. "I declare, Brady Minton," she said. She put a hand on his shoulder. "You're almost as tall as your father. Did you know that?"

Brady didn't feel tall when he got upstairs. When he saw his father lying in bed, he knew it was going to be even harder to talk than he had expected. His father looked like a stranger. A bandage was wound around his forehead, another around his left arm; his right leg was in a splint and propped high on pillows. Part of his face was stubbly from not shaving and the rest of it was white as paper.

"Shut the door, Brady." Even Mr. Minton's voice was different.

Brady shut the door and walked to the middle of the room. He cleared his throat.

"How are you feeling, Pa?" he asked.

He couldn't bear to look at his father, all pieced up

like that with strips of cloth and slats of wood, and his eyes still holding some of the hurt. Brady stared at the floor and waited for his father to speak again. The braided rug that Brady was standing on went around and around his feet in red and white circles.

"Let's get to the point," Mr. Minton said. "What have you got to say for yourself?"

For a minute Brady didn't think he was going to be able to say anything, the way those circles were going around. Then with what seemed an extraordinary amount of effort, he walked over the braided rug to the window. What did he have to say for himself? The way his father had put the question, he didn't have much to say. He looked out the window at the Sermon House showing over the rise of the hill, so small from here, its window no larger than a postage stamp. He did have something to say for the Sermon House. He certainly did. It didn't matter what happened to him; it was the Underground station that mattered. On no account must the line from Parley Potter to Drover Hull be changed or broken. His father must understand. The Sermon House was as safe as it ever was. And so was Drover Hull's cave.

Brady moved over to his father's bed and his words tumbled over themselves in his anxiety to tell the story right, from that first day when he'd come upon the Jerusalem room through the moment Moss Brady had followed Drover Hull down to the river. He had to make his father see. Had to, had to — the words hammered in the back of his head.

When he had finished, Brady walked back to the window. Every word that he knew, he had used. Every feeling he had, he had spent. He leaned his head against the cool glass windowpane.

"Did you tell anyone, Brady? Anyone at all?"

Brady didn't look at his father. "No, sir," he said. In the west, in a rosy flush, the sun was making a last-minute appearance after the gray day. The edges of the hills were stained with pink and gold; lavender feathers swept across the sky. If his father wouldn't trust him, there was only one thing to do, Brady thought. He'd leave. Get out. Go west, that's what he'd do. Then the Underground station in the Sermon House could go on as it had before.

"What did Drover Hull say to you?"

"Said you hadn't trusted me a couple of months ago and a boy doesn't change much in that time." Brady thought how his father must hate having a gawky schoolboy in on a secret he'd kept from his brother Earl, and from Matt, grown men you could trust until doomsday.

"Why did you take Moss last night, Brady? If you'd left him here, I'd never have known about your indiscretion in discovering the station."

Brady sank down on the window seat. Every question his father asked was like a pin sticking into him. "I knew you'd likely be mad at me," Brady admitted dully. "But at the time the important thing seemed to be to get Moss to Uncle Will's. You couldn't carry out the plan and I thought I should do it in your place. I guess I never thought you would maybe want to give up the station because I knew."

Brady sighed and ran his tongue around his lips. There was another reason he'd gone to Uncle Will's. He'd wanted to give Uncle Earl the knife. As long as he was going to Washington, he'd thought he might as well go to Uncle Will's too. But Brady hadn't told his father any of that story — nothing about Laban Williams at all. He took a deep breath and began at the point when he'd crawled out of bed at Matt's boarding-house. As he talked, he thought how silly he sounded — running off, half-cocked, in the middle of the night about one thing or another. "I tried to ask you what to do before I left here with Moss," he finished lamely, "but you were too sick."

Mr. Minton closed his eyes and didn't speak for a minute. When he did, his voice was softer, or perhaps only more tired.

"What do you really think about slavery, son? Do you think it's a bad thing?"

Brady spun around to face his father. A bad thing! This was the last question in the world Brady expected his father to ask. "It's a sin," Brady whispered. "You said so yourself. And I'm going to do something about it. One way or another, sometime when I'm able."

Brady thrust his hands into his pockets, digging deep until he met a crackling sound at the bottom of one pocket. He drew out a piece of paper. It was the letter his Uncle Will had asked Brady to give his father.

Brady stood at the window while his father read the

letter. Maybe his father never would say anything. Maybe he'd never come right out and say, You did right or you did wrong. Or — I'll keep on with the Sermon House or I'll have to close it. This would be the worst.

Mr. Minton folded the letter. "The letter was about you, Brady," he said. "Your Uncle Will said you did a good job."

Brady stepped forward onto the braided rug again. What about you? he wanted to say. How do you feel? But the words stuck on the end of his tongue like cockleburs.

"Brady, I'd like to have the Bible now. Would you bring it to me, please?"

In the half-light of the bedroom, Brady could hardly see his father's face at all. All he could see was his father's stick of a broken leg raised grotesquely in the air. Well, that was that, Brady thought. His father had closed the subject.

"And a candle," Mr. Minton added as Brady started out of the room. His father was going to read the Bible and not say another thing.

Brady put the candle on the table beside his father's bed. The flickering flame set shadows wandering over the wall.

"A pen and ink too, Brady."

Brady went out of the room a second time without thinking about the request one way or another. The text of his father's sermon came to his mind. "There is a time to be silent and a time to speak." This was a time to speak, Brady said to himself. Oh, please let his father speak.

It was not until Brady came back into the room that it occurred to him there was anything strange afoot. Mr. Minton had the Bible opened on the bed beside him and he had twisted his body into the most awkward position, half on his side, in order to be above the Bible and yet not disturb his leg.

"Dip the pen in the ink for me, son," Mr. Minton said.

Brady glanced at the Bible. It was open at the family history page. The last entry was on the day Matt became a professor. Brady felt his heart pounding in his throat. What was his father going to do?

"Hold the candle closer, Brady."

Brady leaned over the bed. The shadows on the wall trembled and flared as he held the candle close.

On this day, Mr. Minton wrote. Each word was written slowly and painstakingly. Brady closed his eyes then, not daring to see what would follow. When he opened them, it was all done.

On this day the barn burned down and Brady Minton did a man's work.

The shadows on the wall danced wildly.

"Of course I can't write down all that you did," Mr. Minton said. "The folks will think this refers to your saving the horses and catching Laban Williams and finding his knife. But you and I will know it means more. A boy becomes a man, Brady, when he finds something outside of himself bigger than he is. Something so important he wants to give himself to it. I believe you've found it. And I'll be expecting you to help me with the Underground while I'm laid up. And when I'm well again, too."

Mr. Minton handed Brady the pen and leaned back on his pillow. "We're in this up to our necks, son, and I don't know where it's going to lead us." He stared out the window across the room, but he didn't appear to be looking at the countryside but at something much farther away.

"One day slavery may be over," Mr. Minton said. "Perhaps when you have sons of your own. When it is, you can look at today's entry and you can add a footnote. 'On this day,' you can write, 'I became a conductor for my father's Underground Railroad station.'" He reached up and patted Brady on the shoulder.

"I'm tired, son," he said. "Blow out the candle and let me rest. Tomorrow we'll have to plan for the harvest and see about putting up a barn."

Brady never remembered going down the stairs that evening. The first thing he knew he was outside, walking down the hill, and Range, on the way up from the pasture, was beside him. The two boys sat down on the steps of the Sermon House. It was dark enough now so that you could barely see the outline of the hills. Already night sounds had replaced day sounds.

"You look mighty happy," Range observed. "What

are you smilin' about? You ben smilin' and smilin' ever since you came out of the house."

"Have I? I didn't know it." Brady was still listening to his father's voice. He went right on smiling foolishly.

"Don't know as I blame you," Range said. "I saw something in town today made me smile too."

"What did you see?" Brady asked the question automatically.

"Laban Williams."

Brady came out of his dream in a hurry and gave Range his full attention.

"Laban had two black eyes," Range went on. "*Two* of them."

Brady grinned. "Real black, were they?"

"They sure were. And you know what I heard?"

"What?"

"I heard you were the one that gave Laban those shiners."

"You heard right."

It was more fun to tell Range the story of Laban and the knife than it had been to tell anyone else. Range became so excited, he had to get up and walk around, and when Brady had finished, Range threw back his head and crowed like a rooster.

"Oh, Brady Minton, you're a humdinger, you are," he cried. "I believe you've rid us of that little polecat once and for all."

When he had finished chortling and cheering about Laban, Range suddenly seemed to be reminded of something. He sat down again and leaned toward Brady as if he were about to share a confidence. "Say, you remember that day we went after blackbirds and I wanted you to go to Drover Hull's cabin and you wouldn't go?"

"I remember."

"You said then you had something to tell me and I never did give you a chance to tell it. That have anything to do with Laban Williams?"

Brady looked up at the sky where the stars were coming out. "No, it didn't."

"What were you goin' to tell me? I've kept wonderin' about it."

Brady didn't say anything.

"Come on, Brady. Tell me."

That whole afternoon came back to Brady as fresh as if it were just over. He could see the redbird falling out of the sky; he could feel the secret burning inside him.

At last Brady spoke.

"You know what that must have been?" he said slowly. "Likely I was going to confess to you how much I dislike hunting. Blackbirds or anything else. Guess I won't do it any more either unless I really need to for one reason or another."

"Is that a fact?"

"Yes."

"Why did you always let on you liked it?"

"I can't think." It was true. For the life of him, Brady couldn't understand why he hadn't told Range before.

All at once Range poked Brady in the ribs. "Well,

why should you shoot, for land's sakes?" he laughed. "Anyone who can punch the way you can don't need to shoot."

Range went home then, still chuckling over a fellow who could land not only one shiner but two in a row.

Brady was on the doorstep of the Sermon House alone. And he was smiling again.

"On this day Brady Minton did a man's work," he whispered. "On this day."

The first faint wispiness of the Milky Way trailed across the sky; the Big Dipper stood boldly in place. And there was the North Star. There it was, all right. Hanging square over Canada. Brady's smile stretched into a grin. That North Star was the brightest thing in the sky, for petey's sakes.